# Use Your
# Jab

Timothy McCain

# USE YOUR
# JAB

## FIGHTING BACK DEPRESSION

# DEDICATION

When God blessed me with an amazing wife and two incredible kids, He was showing off. Madai, you embody strength, grace, power and beauty. You are Krispy Creme when the is light on, and fresh bread rolls from Texas Roadhouse, or simply put, you are perfect. To my son Hezekiah you are the best son in the world and make me continually want to be a better man. To my daughter Brielle, you are the exclamation to the purpose of my life. I love you and will continue to fight for you as you grow up to be a powerful woman full of vision and purpose. Yes, I wear many hats, but no title or responsibilities comes close to being called Husband and Daddy.

In memory of Uncle James J. (Woody) Woodbury

# Endorsements

Some years ago when my own young adult son went through a period of sad, I wish we would have already had this book as a family. Since then we've learned there are real life practical methods, habits and insights available to get control of the fight—through Christ in us—and, there are friends and professionals who understand depression, anxiety and brain biochemistry health. But you have to know how to use your jab, spiritually and practically. Timothy, thank you for sharing and showing us how.

Christopher N. Beard
Lead Pastor, Peoples Church Cincinnati
Author of, <u>Remarkable</u>

I believe there is something greater in each one of us that God wants to draw out, but I also believe there are some things even worse that the enemy of our soul is trying to make way into each one of us. High levels of fear, anxiety and depression are just of a few. Timothy McCain shares how to keep that enemy, not just at bay but also down for the count and has always had a way of communicating truths in dynamic ways and he does it again, masterfully, in "Use Your Jab." Get ready to see how to win the fight for your life.

-David Grieve
Pastor and author of "Son of David: Drawing the king out in every man"


This is the book that you need in your collection right now! Depression is something that many Christians deal with in today's society. The unfortunate reality of this is that the church prescribes prayer and fasting as an antidote to these physical and mental ailments. Prayer and fasting is certainly necessary but there are supplemental things that we need to overcome depression. Pastor Timothy McCain in *Use Your Jab* has masterfully detailed the tactics needed to overcome depression by identifying the four major categories of this issue. Do not waste any further time! Read this now!

Carlos Puentes
Throne of Positivity

Depression and anxiety literally impacts everyone. If you don't suffer from it, someone who is close to you surely does. Timothy McCain, as he's done in previous books, tackles this very big topic and a way that inspires us toward health while giving us practical steps we can take today. "Use Your Jab" is a book that is a must-have for everyone's library. If you're looking to be the healthiest version of YOU, look no further. Discover hope and freedom in "Use Your Jab" and live the life God's always intended for you to have "life to the full"!

-Tim Parsons
Leadership for Work and Home
timparsons.me
@_TimParsons_
facebook.com/timparsonswriter

In reading this book, I have already been comforted in knowing that I am not the only one who goes through an ongoing mental struggle. Depression is a thief that will steal your purpose and the opportunities that life holds for you. Use Your Jab will help you fight and overcome the mental obstacles in your life and so much more.
-Joshua McCain
Worship Artist

"Use Your Jab" is a perfect analogy describing the process of protecting yourself from something that is attempting to do you harm. Depression and anxiety are two very real aspects of mental illness that have taken root in our society like a pestilence looking to devour anything it can if allowed. It is only through the understanding that what your feeling is real, even if it is only real to you, that one my face this challenge. The first part of overcoming mental illness is acknowledging its existence and recognizing its triggers. "Use Your Jab" by Rev. McCain is the perfect tool to add to your toolbelt aiding in reconstructing your life and enabling you to reach your fullest, most fantastic potential.

-Dr. Eric C. Ortiz

# TABLE OF CONTENTS

# ACKNOWLEDGMENTS

Thank you to everyone that has continued to support me throughout the years. Thank you for the encouraging words, support, prayers, friendship, and much more. Thank you to my family, that is blood and the family that I gained that I get to call friends. Massive shoutout to those that support us monthly as we couldn't do what we do without yall. Thank you to the Singer, Stensland, Revilla, Arevalo, and Riveria families, as I have no idea where I would be in my life without yall. If I name everyone that has been apart of my journey, that would be another book in and of itself, and I would hate to miss someone. So allow me the grace to tell you all, thank you.

# CHAPTER 1

## WHEN-WIN

My uncle, James J. Woody, was a professional boxer from 1964-1976. He fought in the heavyweight division in a southpaw stance. Born in the Bronx, New York, he was able to travel all around, putting on his boxing gloves and fighting off opponents. One of his most renowned opponents that he fought against was the Heavy Weight Champion named George Foreman. I wish I could go back in time and sit in the stands just to see my uncle box in his prime. I can imagine hearing the shouts from the corner telling him to stay on the outside of the orthodox foot so he can have an advantage as a southpaw. Hearing his coaches passionately yell at him to keep his hands up and protect himself. If Mrs. Frizzle from the Magic School Bus was real, I would be calling her to take a trip back in time to be in awe of a man living out his dreams fighting on the canvas.

Boxing is a sport that may look easy watching it from the comfort of a couch, but it is a very technical and taxing sport. There are many punches to throw, but you must know which one to throw at the correct time. If you throw a hook at the wrong time, leaving yourself open, you may get laid out and knocked down. It is a technical sport that involves defense and offense continually. The three-minute rounds may feel like an eternity as your body is being pushed to its limits. However, even with all of this and more, I love the "sweet science of boxing."

A few years ago, I decided to pursue boxing for myself, and it has been a journey that has helped me not only physically, mentally but also emotionally, and in some ways spiritually. I am six foot six inches tall, and I weigh around 320 pounds. I am a southpaw boxer with a long reach and a strong jab. When I started boxing at my home gym called "Deland Boxing," the coaches would tell the class repeatedly how vital the jab is in boxing. I always thought that boxing was about knocking someone out, but it is more complicated than that. Boxing is more than the hook and a strong right hand. It is more than uppercuts and power shots but its footwork, endurance, and distance management. For a boxer, the most essential and vital punch a boxer needs to master is the jab. Jabbing is like dribbling in basketball; it is how you get positioned to score and win. When sparring, my coaches would tell me repeatedly to use the jab or stay behind the jab. Why? There are many reasons, but one of the reasons being it makes sure your opponent is not going to get in the inside. I have a long reach, so if I use my jab correctly, they wouldn't be able to get close enough to land a shot. So, with footwork and constantly throwing the jab, I will be able to stay in the fight, score points, and when the right time comes, land power shots. The purpose of the jab is to make sure what is on the outside of you doesn't get in the inside of you.

**Stay behind the jab**

You may be reading all of this and be asking what does any of this have to do with or apply to my life? I am not writing this book to encourage you to learn how to box or how to throw a punch. However, knowing how to emotionally and spiritually use your jab against the toxic influences in your life is vital to keep you standing and in the fight of life. Depression, worry, and stress are in the ring of life at the same time, and knowing how to stay behind your jab, standing on God's word, practicing healthy behaviors is going to help you win. When depression, worry, fear, and other binding emotions get in the inside of you, it throws heavy punches that brings you down to your knees. It can keep you in your bed in the morning because you don't want to face the day. It will taunt you with fear so you lose your desire to chase after your dreams. It will swing wild punches that you didn't see coming as thoughts to hurt yourself or leave everything bombards your thought life.

Right now, as I am writing this book, COVID-19, also known as the Coronavirus, is impacting the entire world in some way. Many have already died, and many are sick, laid up in hospital beds. Businesses were forced to close, and mandatory stay at home orders were placed. We are practicing social distancing as recommended by government officials and staying six feet apart from everyone. Many people lost their jobs and living in a place of uncertainty that is shaking them to the core. It can seem as if life is falling apart, and everything you worked so hard for is crashing down in the span of a couple of months. This is a high level of stress that, if left unchecked, will overtake and overwhelm many. For some, the stay-at-home orders may feel like a vacation, while for others, it may feel like a death sentence. Leaving your house to go to work or school was an escape from the toxic dysfunction that happens behind closed doors. It was a reprieve of rest from the drinking, yelling, and fighting, but now you may feel like there is nowhere to go to escape the pain that is normal in your household. The struggle that many are facing during this time is real, and we must learn how to fight and to stand. What do you do when the bills are stacking up, yet funds aren't coming in? How do you handle the stress of school being closed, and now you are trying to be a teacher and a mother? How do you process the moment you got notice that you have the virus and now must self-quarantine yourself from your family completely? How do you manage the stress of being on the frontlines in the medical field, combating this invisible enemy that is snatching the lives of people both young and old? **Depression and deep sadness rides on the back of stress attempting to make an unattested entry into your heart.** It desires to get in the inside of you because if it can get in your heart and establish itself in your thought life, it will give fear its marching orders and overwhelm you. Use your jab and fight off the depression, stress, worry, and other venomous emotions attempting to poison your heart and mind. Keep your hands up, use your jab, and as the referees tell the boxers seconds before they face-off, "protect yourself at all times".

Proverbs 4:20-27 (NIV)

**20** My son, pay attention to what I say;
  turn your ear to my words.
 **21** Do not let them out of your sight,
  keep them within your heart;
**22** for they are life to those who find them
  and health to one's whole body.
**23** *Above all else, guard your heart,*
  *for everything you do flows from it.*
**24** Keep your mouth free of perversity;
  keep corrupt talk far from your lips.
**25** Let your eyes look straight ahead;
  fix your gaze directly before you.
**26** Give careful thought to the paths for your feet
  and be steadfast in all your ways.
**27** Do not turn to the right or the left;
  keep your foot from evil.

Life can be overwhelming at times and can feel like an uphill battle. The fight is to make sure that what is happening on the outside of you doesn't get into the inside of you. Proverbs 4:23 encourages us to guard and protect our hearts, and this is vital we do just that. Why? Because if the wellspring of your heart is poisoned, then everything that draws and drinks from that well will be contaminated. Toddlers will drink tainted waters from their sippy cups given by their parents yelling at them for reasons beyond their control. Wives and husbands will get the brunt of condescending words as the mismanagement of stress occurs from the pressure of being jobless. Bottles and drugs will become demanded by unlicensed psychologists and therapists as teens and adults alike self-medicate feelings and emotions. Protecting yourself is vital if you expect to survive the fight and combat the brawl of depression and stress.

**FOOTWORK**

An encouraging truth that we must remember during this time of uncertainty is that this didn't take God by surprise. Before He spoke the world into existence, He knew of this day, and He is aware of how to get you through it. Sometimes the fight in and of itself is surviving to the next round and the next day. The struggle during the combat of emotional hostility is to remain standing during and when the fight is happening.

Ephesians 6:10-18 (NIV)

**10** Finally, be strong in the Lord and in his mighty power. **11** Put on the full armor of God, so that you can take your stand against the devil's schemes. **12** For our struggle is not against flesh and blood, but against the rulers, against the authorities, against the powers of this dark world and against the spiritual forces of evil in the heavenly realms. **13** Therefore put on the full armor of God, so that **when** the day of evil comes, you may be able to stand your ground, and after you have done everything, to stand. **14** Stand firm then, with the belt of truth buckled around your waist, with the breastplate of righteousness in place, **15** and with your feet fitted with the readiness that comes from the gospel of peace. **16** In addition to all this, take up the shield of faith, with which you can extinguish all the flaming arrows of the evil one. **17** Take the helmet of salvation and the sword of the Spirit, which is the word of God. **18** And pray in the Spirit on all occasions with all kinds of prayers and requests. With this in mind, be alert and always keep on praying for all the Lord's people.

We are in a fight and have always been in one whether we are aware of it or not. It is encouraging to know that Jesus didn't leave us abandoned or powerless to be an overcomer. Paul, the writer of Ephesians, gives attention to the fight and instructs us to wear the armor of God. In my book "Crowns are Greater Than Trophies" in a chapter called "Crowned with Victory," I write in more detail about each individual armor. I strongly encourage you to read this book during this time to reinforce your effort to fight and conquer the battles you are facing today.

This fight doesn't take God by surprise, in fact, He even warned us in verse 13, stating that "when" the day of evil comes, not if or I wonder but when. We need to be thankful for the sunshine and the easy days but also be prepared for the times that storms roll in and the moments when hurricanes of life blow against the lives that were built. I firmly believe that the fight in and of itself is standing. By standing and doing whatever it takes to stand gives notion to remain in the fight even though it is hard. In boxing, your footwork is just as important as your punches. A great boxer knows the importance of having strong legs and a stable foundation to throw punches. The stabilization of your legs can be directly connected to the efficiency of your punches. When the bell is rung for the first round of the fight, they start with fresh legs and maybe you don't give much attention to them. However, in the later rounds, you can see their legs beginning to lose strength and endurance. The fighter, whose energy is being depleted, will start to move slower, and instead of stepping into the punch, now they are leaning, leaving their chin exposed, setting the stage to be knocked out.

The fight is tiring, draining, and hard, there is no doubt about that, which is why you must train for the later rounds before the match, so you have the conditioning necessary to survive and thrive in the later rounds of the fight. The times when your shoulders feel like boulders, so you keep dropping your hands and lowering your guard. The times that you are fighting to catch your breath and having a hard time throwing a good jab. The work you do before the bell is rung will help you to win and be an overcomer. When I first started to box, my cardiovascular condition was very poor. Yes, I can punch hard and move fast for others by size, but my tank would run out fast. When I lost all my energy, I discovered that I would throw fewer jabs or move less because I was tired beyond belief. My coach confronted me and told me that I couldn't reach the next level if I am not conditioned. He put me on a workout plan to run three 5k's a week, and it turned my life around. I discovered that the work I did on the outside of the ring prepared me to win on the inside of the ring. I was able to stand and keep standing in the fight because of the discipline I acquired before the fight ever started.

I don't know what your fight looks like or the battles you have been fighting. However, I can assume that it is tiring and difficult. I firmly believe that you can WIN WHEN your day of evil comes. You will WIN WHEN your WHEN happens. Your "When" are your hardships, struggles, battles in and on every arena of conflict, whether physically, mentally, emotionally, or spiritually. You will WIN WHEN your day of evil comes. God hasn't forsaken you, and He is cheering for you in your corner. I can hear Him now coaching to slip when depression whispers lies in your direction. Jesus is telling you to roll as a wild hook of fear is trying to knock you down.

Keep standing on God's promises that say He fights for you because you aren't alone. Jesus is in your corner, continually shouting "Use your jab" so you can make sure what is on the outside of you doesn't get in the inside of you. You will WIN WHEN your "when" happens.

# CHAPTER 2

## JUST SMILE

"You should smile more" are the words many people who are going through deep sadness and depression will frequently hear. Yet, in the same way, the person who is always smiling and wanting to make others laugh may be the one fighting back depression at every waking moment. Depression doesn't always look like the person with a frown, wrapped in the blanket, refusing to leave their bed. In fact, they may be the most outgoing person in public yet, cries themselves to sleep every night. It's an unwelcomed guest that refuses to leave the house when the party is over, unlike sadness, which knows to leave when happiness rings the doorbell. Depression can care less about your resume, title, or position of power. It shows up when everything is going right and can compound when it seems like everything is going wrong. It's a gas-guzzling vehicle of worry that's quickly driving its passengers off a cliff of fear, anxiety, and hopelessness.

It seems to be that the antidote others may have for people going through depression is just to smile. But the problem with this is that an outward expression may not fix an inward circumstance. In the same way, one will never tell a disabled person in a wheelchair to put shoes on as if it's the remedy to help them walk. It is easier to fight battles that are publicly tangible and easier to recognize, than it is to bring healing to a problem no one can see or feel but the host itself. Depression and deep sadness have been a taboo subject for quite a long time, especially in church. We have dealt with depression in church one too many times strictly from a spiritual standpoint. Even though I believe it is vital to recognize the spiritual dynamics of depression, anxiety, and worry, this cannot be the only front in which this war is being waged.

## WAR

In a time of war and battle, the Marines, Army, Navy, Airforce and Coast Guard may all be called upon, even one at a time, staggered or all at once. All of the brave men and women have the same fight, yet each of them is skilled in different battlefields to win the same war. If there are enemy jets flying around seeking to destroy lives, it is not the Marines shooting AR-15 rifles from the ground, but the Air Force also flying its jets to take out the enemy. The fight is the same, but the battlegrounds are different. For so long, the fight against depression from the church has often times been on the wrong battlefield and even though the intentions are good, many are losing their lives. Not because they didn't have the will to fight but because the methods were not aligned.

Personally, this was a hard concept for me to wrap my head around at first, because I believed and still believe in the raw power of God. I have witnessed God do signs wonders and miracles, time and time again. In our ministry, we have seen thousands upon thousands give their lives to Jesus, and it never gets old. I hold what God can do, with just one-touch with great high esteem, and when I was younger in ministry, I truly believed that all those going through depression or deep sadness, just needed a Marine-like encourager at the altar. Yet, I noticed that after the tears, the shouts and experience, some still struggled with the same issue. Could it be that depression could and should be fought on all different battlegrounds to beat it? Never taking away from a touch from God and the power of His Word, as it becomes the infantry of truth marching into the heart of the believer, but maybe the Navy needs to be called because it is those ships that are equipped with therapists that know how to talk and ask questions to the wounded warrior and get to the root of the issues. Or perhaps the Coast Guard needs to be utilized to help save the person drowning in anger, loneliness, and blame due to the unresolved crisis and childhood trauma. Could it be that the Army is on a rescue mission to help free trapped victims in the midst of war to help them navigate the practical things to do for self-care and reasonable steps to achieve emotional and nutritional balance? All the while, never forgetting the real and raw reality that we are in spiritual warfare and some may be POW's in a demonic struggle, and we need the Marines to kick down the enemy's doors, cast out every controlling spirit and liberate the captive. Once again, all of these are important and if we are going to see healing in the area of depression we cannot only shout at it, we must talk about it. Some people may need both a pastor and a therapist and that is ok. It doesn't mean you are less of a Christian, or you have less faith. In the same way, many diabetic Christians are walking the earth today. They may serve God with all of their hearts and still take insulin shots to live, whereas some people with depression may have a chemical imbalance for which holistic or pharmaceutical means may drastically help.

**Put on the Gloves**

Maybe you are going through depression, and if you are, I am glad you are reading this book right now. You have been told to learn how to cope with it, but I want to encourage you to learn how to fight through it. There is a fight in you that is going to amaze you. Could it be that the reason you, solely, just accepted a lifestyle of deep sadness and depression, that you have thought it is a permanent solitary-confinement in which you have placed yourself on? You made an effort in the past and got hit, thus told yourself that you couldn't win the fight. If you have entertained that thought, I am glad to tell you that getting hit isn't a sign that you can't win, in fact, it is the sign that the fight is still going on. In boxing, the opponent can't hit a fighter that is laid out on the canvas, but they can swing towards one that is still standing. You may have been knocked down, but you are still in the fight. Watch your footwork, think about your breathing and use your jab to keep your opponent of depression at bay. Use your reach, and if it keeps trying to get inside, use that check hook. There is a fighter in you, and you still have a chance to win.

You have seen depressions' highlight reels, and you know when it is going to throw a punch or slip. You have already taken the hardest punch it can throw yet you are still standing. But in order to win, you are going to have to score some points or knock it out. You can't just slip and weave out of shots, but you are going to have to punch back and learn how to counter. Maybe for the first few rounds, you stood there and took a beating, but enough is enough. It capitalizes on the moments that you drop your guard or get distracted. Study your enemy, its triggers and patterns, so you can learn how to avoid the hit and take the fight to it. You may have gotten hit, but the fight is still far from over.

In the following chapters, I am going to take you to a training camp so you can be better prepared to fight depression. Depression doesn't fight fair, so it always asks anxiety and worry about coming along, but don't stress, because you are going to overcome them too.

## The Playbook

I have categorized depression in four parts to explain the roots better and give suggestions on how to overcome them. The categories are: Chemical, Trauma, Circumstantial, and Spiritual.

Chemical has to do with the hormonal imbalances in our bodies that may place some to be greatly predisposed to depression. Trauma and crisis are the defining moments to pain, despair, and tragedy that may be a root of the tree in which you have been eating depressions' fruit. Circumstantial will be talking about the different seasons in our lives and how to combat them. For many people, even though they may not have been diagnosed with depression, they may find themselves in this tug of war. Lastly, Spiritual is an important category that needs to be addressed as the enemy is very real, and it still out to rob, kill, and destroy.

Depression is very real, and it isn't something to just overlook or think it will go away with time. It must be confronted, and it must be healed. It requires more than just hearing a well-intended person telling you to "just smile". It is going to need you to consistently and conscientiously fight against it. "Ding," the bell has just rung. It is time to get out of your corner and fight, but just remember to use your jab.

# CHAPTER 3

## SHADOWBOXING

**M**ental Health is a battle that is hard to fight for many people because the wounds and struggles aren't as always physically recognizable. Hypertension, also known as high blood pressure, has been called the "silent killer." Many have called it by that name because a person can have it and feel totally fine. It doesn't show up on their skin like a lump that needs to be checked out. There are limited outward identifiers that can lead a person to become a believer that they need to seek help or a loving person to notice that they need it.

In the same way, issues with mental health doesn't always fit into the stereotype and is often times fictionally portrayed as those images that we see in movies. It may not be the extreme of a person in a straitjacket whispering unrecognizable words, even though there are some fighting that battle. However, issues of mental health don't have a face, it has many faces. This notion adds to the complication of ushering a remedy to the afflicted minds because, for some, if they can't see it, then it's not real or an issue at all. Many people don't believe that it is real, so the moment someone dealing with a mental illness or even the intense feelings that follow it, people think they're overreacting or it is not a big deal. Thus, compounds to the frustration of knowing that there may be something wrong, but no one will believe them, as the taboo of mental health is still alive and well.

Consequently, people with the struggle stay silent because, at least then, they are safe from the verbal thrown stones of uncompassionate or ignorant people. However, if a person will say that they have diabetes, there is an understanding of the importance of insulin. Depression, anxiety, and other mental struggles can be affected and caused by chemical imbalances in a person's body. It is essential to understand that some symptoms outwardly may have roots inwardly. For too long, there has been a taboo that mental health issues, depression, and other problems like this meant a person is weak, and something is wrong with them as a person, rather than the possibility that something is sick in their body that needs healing.

In professional boxing matches, the fighters are aware of who their opponent is for the upcoming fight night. In fact, they have quite a long time to prepare for the battle.

Knowing precisely who they are fighting, they spend a lot of time learning about them. Are they an aggressive boxer who continually moves forward or do they box from the back foot? Do they use a Peek-a-boo stance or a Philly Shell? Are they southpaw or orthodox in their stance? They are aware of the other stats, arms reach, and details. A great boxer and team will study the fighter so they will know and discover ways to win and be effective in the ring. It is vital that we learn how to do the same things so we can fight and confront the taboo and stigmas of depression, anxiety, and mental illness that may stem from chemical imbalances.

## Tyson Fury

One of my top five favorite boxers is a man named who defeated Wladimir Klitschko named Tyson Fury. He is a 6' 9" heavyweight champion that has fought on and off the ring. My respect for this man is unmeasurable, hearing his story and triumphs with mental illness such as depression, anxiety and panic attacks. As an author, I can't believe I am telling you this, but I encourage you to put this book down right now. Open up YouTube and search for Tyson Fury's interview on showtime called *"Tyson Fury on Mental Health & Recovery | Full Interview | Showtime boxing."* In this interview with sports announcer, Mauro Ranallo, they begin to pull down the curtain of a lot of misconceptions and confusion about mental health. Honesty, please, check it out before you continue to read, as less than an hour of your time could change your life forever.

Fury had everything a boxing champion could dream of,

from belts, wealth, fame, and family. However, he felt like he gained the entire world but was broken and empty inside. He was around places where happiness should have been present yet, he felt alone, isolated, and depressed. He is not the stereotypical image of mental health that people wrongfully carried but a large, powerful man struggling with an invisible enemy bringing him down to his knees. In his interview, he shares raw and honest information about how he felt daily, that he wanted to die. He discovered that he would get moments of relief when he was drinking, as it temporarily numbed the pain he felt inside. However, every single day when the bottles were empty, and he got sober, the problem was still present. He gained loads of weight, the family was in disarray, doing hard drugs, lost his belts, and was staring rock bottom face to face. Many people counted him out as a lost cause, turn their back on him, and assumed that he was a washed-up person who just lacked self-control. Yet, there was an underlining monster causing a rampage in his mind telling him that he didn't need a hero to help him confront his condition and the discipline to shut the door so the onslaught could end. In his interview, he shared about a turnaround moment on Halloween when he stood in front of life's' mirror and finally looked back. He left the party he was at and went back home. Suddenly he found himself in a room crying out to God. He shared that he wept and wept asking God to take the burden off of him. He acknowledged that he was doing it alone and needed His help. After that encounter with the Lord in prayer, he went downstairs and told his wife that he was turning his life around. **It is paramount to see that and understand that his time in prayer didn't just lead him to a notion or theory, but to action.** The next day he put on his running shoes and attempted to run two miles but couldn't make it, so he walked the rest of the distance. He called a team together to start training again and made up in his mind that he was going to gain everything back that he lost. At the writing of this book, he lived up to this dream and is once again an undefeated Heavy Weight Champion of the world after fighting another boxer I admire named Deontay Wilder, who also overcame many adversities to get where he is in life.

Tyson Fury understood many truths about his fight with mental health that we should all take note of. He realized that he had to get professional help and get guidance on how to treat what he was dealing with. If a person is deathly sick, they understand that they head to the Emergency Room to get better, not to the auto-mechanic. Knowing where to go for help and having the strength to do it is vital as this helps you keep the fight alive to overcome depression, anxiety, and whatever is in your ring of life. Secondly, Fury built a team and community of people around him that not only encouraged and challenged him but held him accountable to his exercise regime and diet. Tyson Fury understood and believed he was going to have to exercise for the rest of his life to jab back the depression, anxiety, and mental battles. In the past, alcohol was his escape of the pain, now exercise is part of his healing. It would be a disservice if I didn't acknowledge the strength and power it has to have a relationship with Jesus. As a Christian, he knew that at all times, he could come to the Lord in prayer. He wasn't fighting alone, but God was fighting with him. He put his trust in God's hands and did what he knew that he needed to do.

If you believe that you have an imbalance in your body that is affecting your mental health, I encourage you to seek professional help and advice. Many things can help the hormones in your body to get back in alignments, such as sleep, exercise, diet, and other practices that don't call for medication. However, I am not qualified to tell you to stop taking or to start taking medication. Discovering holistic approaches and lifestyle changes that can add to your healing of mental health is also a significant step to take in the fight that I highly recommended.

Jesus died and hung on the cross for us to be made whole in every aspect of life. He died for our salvation but also for our healing, among many other things. The oversight that people can make is assuming that the healing that the Word of God refers to is just for the physical issues of a person's body. This incomplete notion can be an unintentional attempt to restrain the depth of His sacrifice. On the contrary, Jesus is after every aspect of our lives that is unhealthy, broken, and out of alignment. His divine approach to healing wasn't singular but multifaceted as its gaze on your mental and emotional well-being. Jesus knows what it is like to be rejected and cast aside. He is aware of the burdens we carry as he bore our sufferings. When He hung on the cross of Calvary, I believe He thought of you and the battle you are fighting right now.

*Isaiah 53:3-5 (NIV)*

*3 He was despised and rejected by mankind,*
*    a man of suffering, and familiar with pain.*
*Like one from whom people hide their faces*
*    He was despised, and we held him in low esteem.*
*4 Surely he took up our pain*
*    and bore our suffering,*
*yet we considered him punished by God,*
*    stricken by him, and afflicted.*
*5 But he was pierced for our transgressions,*
*    he was crushed for our iniquities;*
*the punishment that brought us peace was on him,*
*    and by his wounds we are healed.*

## Shadow Boxing

In boxing, there is a practice and routine that is a must in every fighter called Shadowboxing. It is when you are fighting in the open without an opponent practicing all of your boxing moves. You are slipping punches that aren't physically being thrown at you and block hooks that are not actually there. You are making sure to be using all of your footwork, head motion and everything you know as you fight the air. To other people that have no idea what Shadowboxing is, you can look like a crazy person punching the air. But the fighter is actually visualizing an opponent in front of them and applying the disciplines of the craft of boxing to do it. In shadow boxing the fight that you are winning on the inside of you makes you a better boxer. I feel this same way when it comes to boxing and fighting the unseen fight of chemical imbalances. To others, it may look like you are crazy and just boxing the air, but you are fighting an invisible enemy. You need to know that Shadowboxing is not a waste of time but a skill and craft that needs to be practiced often. I want to encourage you to keep fighting that enemy that no one else can see, but you see staring you down every single day. Use your jab and fight back panic attacks and anxiety as you go throughout your day. You aren't boxing a shadow. You're fighting an issue that you must be brave enough to seek help if you need it.

Not every person that is depressed has a mental illness or a chemical imbalance. But if you are the person that falls in the category, lace your gloves up and hire a personal coach that will be in your corner helping you win this fight. Whether that is a doctor or a lifestyle change or all of the above, it is vital that you don't ignore it anymore and stop standing as a heavy bag when you have to ability to fight back. Tyson Fury is a hero for many people and an example of how you can rise up out of the depths of depression, anxiety, and other imbalances, and stand with both arms up in victory knowing you have once again dared to fight. If you are reading this and your depression, panic attacks, and other battles are medically connected, then please seek proper help and guidance. Confront the taboo of mental health and punch it square in the face because it needs to stop getting in your way to healing. You are a fighter and you are a winner, so stand back up and get back in the fight.

# CHAPTER 4

## COVER UP

Boxing is a sport that demands everything from you before, during, and after the fight in the ring. How you train before the fight weighs heavy as you are squared up waiting for the bell to ring. It's the overlooked and non-glamorous disciplines and exercises that set a person apart from each other. Having a cardiovascular engine that can go the distance is vital to staying in the fight. When you get tired, you get lazy with your footwork, throwing wild punches and quick to neglect to cover yourself. All it takes is one punch at the right place at the correct time to put you to sleep and eating the canvas. The next thing you know, it's the punch you didn't see coming that becomes your lullaby rocking, or should I say knocking you to sleep. When you are fighting tired, protecting yourself in a fight becomes a daunting task. It can feel that your mind is telling you to do the thing that your body has a hard time keeping up. The fight against depression, deep sadness, and anxiety can feel like you are fighting tired. As if heavy stones were tied to your wrist, slowing down every motion and effort. You are trying your best, but it's like something is impeding your work and sapping your energy. If left unchecked, you know that it wouldn't matter how much wishful thinking you can muster up; failure will be the result.

Right before the two opponents go to their designated corners of the ring, the referee tells them to touch gloves and "protect themselves at all times." Win or lose, every athlete and coach review the tapes to understand why the outcome happened. There is an understanding that in order to move forward, you must look backward. To keep winning or to start, there needs to be moments when you check the records to understand what went wrong. As you are fighting back depression it may be highly likely that you need to review, to play times of your life and childhood. Unchecked and unresolved Crisis and Trauma is fighting with your hands behind your back without gas in the tank to withstand the beating. While studying depression, I came across one of the most educating and informative TED Talks I have ever heard. Every word had me nodding my head, seeing how all the dots were connected to childhood trauma and physical and mental health. Before you read any further, put this book down and pull up Youtube. Search "How childhood trauma affects health across a lifetime" by

Pediatrician Dr. Nadine Burke Harris. Mark this place in the book and take 16:03 minutes and watch the video. Dr. Harris opens up about in the mid-90s, the CDC-Kaiser Permanente released and studied the information connected to 7 out of the 10 leading causes of death. Like a hook reeling in the listeners with every word, she states that it can affect the immune system, brain development, triple the risk of heart and lung disease, and even cause a 20-year life expectancy gap. You may assume that it was some chemical or toxin, but it is, in fact, the exposure to childhood trauma. A test was created called the Adverse Childhood Experience that would help create a point system to measure the trauma and crisis a person experienced. Every point they gained in the ACE score would be correlated to health outcomes connected to trauma responses. Directly from the CDC website, yes, the CDC, the Center for Disease Control and Prevention, there is a wealth of knowledge and information on ACE's CDC website. Here is how it describes and categorizes different traumas and crises that they can undergo before 18 years old.

## "ACEs Definitions

- *Abuse*

    - ***Emotional abuse:*** *A parent, stepparent, or adult living in your home swore at you, insulted you, put you down, or acted in a way that made you afraid that you might be physically hurt.*

    o **Physical abuse:** *A parent, stepparent, or adult living in your home pushed, grabbed, slapped, threw something at you, or hit you so hard that you had marks or were injured.*

    o **Sexual abuse:** *An adult, relative, family friend, or stranger who was at least 5 years older than you ever touched or fondled your body in a sexual way, made you touch his/her body in a sexual way, attempted to have any type of sexual intercourse with you.*

- *Household Challenges*

    o **Mother treated violently:** *Your mother or stepmother was pushed, grabbed, slapped, had something thrown at her, kicked, bitten, hit with a fist, hit with something hard, repeatedly hit for over at least a few minutes, or ever threatened or hurt by a knife or gun by your father (or stepfather) or mother's boyfriend.*

    o **Substance abuse in the household:** *A household member was a problem drinker or alcoholic or a household member used street drugs.*

    o **Mental illness in the household:** *A household member was depressed or mentally ill or a household member attempted suicide.*

    o **Parental separation or divorce:** *Your parents were ever separated or divorced.*

    o **Incarcerated household member:** *A household member went to prison.*

- o [https://www.cdc.gov/violencepreve ntion/aces/about.html?CDC_AA_refVal=htt ps%3A%2F%2Fwww.cdc.gov%2Fviolencepre vention%2Facestudy%2Fabout.html](https://www.cdc.gov/violenceprevention/aces/about.html?CDC_AA_refVal=https%3A%2F%2Fwww.cdc.gov%2Fviolenceprevention%2Facestudy%2Fabout.html)

Pediatrician Nadine Burke gave remarkable stats such as 67% of the population had at least one ACE. She continued to state how 12.6% had four or more points. There was a clear correlation with the response to the outcome of a person's health. For example, a person with four or more points was 2 1/2 times more likely to have Chronic obstructive pulmonary disease and hepatitis than a person that scored a zero in the test. The ACE test stated for the risk of depression, it is 4 1/2 times more likely than a person with a score of zero. Also, the risk of suicide was 12 times more likely than a person with a zero score. If someone had a seven or more score, they had a triple risk of lung cancer and was even 3 1/2 times more likely to have the number one killer in the United States, Ischemic heart disease. These are not just random facts or assumptions that she was sharing but results backed up by science. According to the study, those with early adverse trauma, affect children's physical development in their brains. The trauma can affect the Nucleus Accumbens in the brain that is the reward center and pleasure connected to substance dependency. It involves the Prefrontal Cortex, which is vital for impulse control, and the Executive Functions with which a cognitive process needed to control behavior and effects learning. Dr. Nadine Burke Harris continues to share about results from MRI scans showing trackable and measurable differences in the Amygdala, which connects to the brain's process of emotions such as fear. I watched and re-watched her Ted Talk over and over, gleaning from the information shared in such an articulate manner. Like a great point guard on a basketball court, she called out the play to set up the alley- oop for a slamdunk. Her illustration of the bear in the woods is fantastic, and I highly suggest watching the video to hear it.

## Get Over It

The question at hand is, where does all of this come into play in our lives? For many of us, we have been taught that ignoring the problem means it is going to go away. Time doesn't fix the issues; it just allows them to fester and destroy. Whatever we don't confront, we allow, and whatever we allow, we accept. What if the depression, anxiety, and chronic sadness is connected to the unchecked and unhealed trauma in your life? You may believe that it doesn't affect you because it was a long time ago, but that may be false. Maybe you were told over and over to get over it, and thus you tried. You coached yourself that as long as you don't feel the pain anymore, then the crisis and trauma won't touch you. Don't get over it; you need to get through it, which happens by confronting it. You remember what it was like to get woken up from your sleep when you were a child to the thunder of yelling and screaming from parents on the verge of divorce. You remember your mom or dad's conversations telling you how horrible each other was, forgetting that just because they are no longer husband and wife, it doesn't mean that they aren't still your mom and dad. They may have separated their affections from each other, but it shouldn't cost you your bond to them. You remember the awful and tragic time you were sexually abused, and every time you tried to tell your story, no one would believe you. You shared the moments when the molester would sneak into your room, to know, to see their face at family events, replaying the images over and over in your mind, reliving it at every sight of their face. You had your fair share of racist encounters and were beaten and made fun of due to your skin color. Countless other issues have robbed you of your innocence. You are growing up to be an adult or even an adult now, and still, as you close your eyes, you can see every detail of your traumatic moments. Have you emotionally, physically, mentally, or spiritually dropped an anchor in your timeline? Like a boat with its anchor in the water trying to move forward, it just takes laps around that moment. You may not think that it isn't a massive problem, but it is festering out of the temporary and futile makeshift bandages of neglect placed over it. Have you taken the time to heal and grieve from the broken marriage? I have had countless families in my office due to dysfunction in their household. Children of divorce have told me that they feel like their parents treat them differently because they look more like the parent that divorced them. Have you been taught to get over it, ignore it, and act like it isn't there or never happened? What if your depression and deep sadness have been an emotional virus using your unchecked trauma as a host to sustain itself throughout all the years of your life? **Ignorance is not a fruit of the spirit. Out of sight and out of mind is not a faith tactic but a coping mechanism.**

**Put'em Back In The Mailbox**.

My dad and I used to watch a show together called *Sanford and Son*. The show is about a father and son who own and operate a junkyard business. In one episode, they are discussing unpaid bills, and now they are being sued. Fred, which is the father's recommendation to his son, was to "put'em back in the mailbox". Sharing his thought process is that if you put it back in the mailbox and don't open the bill, it never got to you, and you don't have to pay it. But as silly as this sounds, if we are not intentional, we can treat our trauma and crisis this same way. It creates a false sense of peace not rooted in legitimate truth. The fact of the matter you can continue to try to put the power bills of your trauma back in the mailbox, but you will find, one day and through life, you will live in the darkness that neglect has created. These issues not only affect you but everyone around you. In my book "Crowns Are Greater Than Trophies," takes a deeper dive into matters like these, that are paramount, matters you need to face before your children are forced to confront it. *"Voluntarily or involuntarily through the hardships of life, we as parents, coaches, mentors, and other voices can stack weights on the backs of children who are not strong enough to carry them. It is in times of anger, selfishness, and other blinding emotions that some tend to lose sight of this truth. The integrity of a child's capacity to handle life situations is often overlooked as we place our worries on them. They then become the collateral damage of internal war—POWs of an external battle and the hostages of emotional conflict. In the time that we are called to steward their precious lives, we can allow our pain to be our professor and seat them in the classroom of our crisis as they take notes gathered from the offense amassed in the shadow of grief. As the saying goes "hurt people hurt people." Pages 116-117*

Crisis and trauma are moments in your life that mark you so deeply that it affects who you are. It scars you so profoundly that you view life differently via the lens of your pain, both subconsciously and intentionally. The fact of the matter is that unresolved issues allow unchallenged problems.

## Sweet Science of Boxing

So much of boxing happens outside of the ring, and it isn't glamorous or, at times, fun. The long hours of intense training, grunting through challenging workouts, build your body and mind. There is a saying which states, " the sweet science of boxing". It isn't throwing random punches hurling towards the opponent's face but executed and intentional choices in the heat of the moment. If you ever watched a boxing match, you can hear the commentators describing the fighters. You will listen to words like he or she is a puncher or a boxer. Every boxer knows how to throw a punch, but not every puncher is skilled at boxing. Of course, you have a knockout artist and punchers like "Butterbean" that wasn't dancing around the ring but used his mass and strength as an artist, throwing timed shots and putting people down to sleep. But then you have boxers like Floyd Mayweather that is a boxer using rounds the learn each opponent. Later into the fight, capitalizing on the holes, openings, or mistakes they are making. Some of the best boxers are scientists of the sport throwing shots to form a hypothesis. When they find out that they keep missing or getting it blocked, they go back to the drawing board. To win, it takes skill, talent, effort, commitment, and heart. This may be true in the different areas of your life: the arenas where your conflict occurs.

Your depression, chronic sadness, fear, the anxiety of other debilitating feelings has been studying you since you were young. It knows how to hit you where it hurts, and when you are down. But how do you get the upper hand? It would help if you learned how to fight back. Go back and study the trauma and crisis in your life that may be the root of so many issues you are facing. You have been rounds and rounds, years and years in the fighting and you are tired. You are dropping your cover but keep your hands up and protect yourself.

## Get a Coach

You may need to seek further help to help you navigate your childhood or even adult trauma. After all, boxers have coaches and teams around them, yelling from the ropes, supporting them to last in the fight and win. When you are physically sick, you see a doctor without question, but what if you need emotional healing? I believe that the expression "worrying yourself sick" isn't an exaggeration but very real. Emotional and mental issues can fester up to be physical problems. Finding a therapist, psychologist, life coach, or all of these above and more can shift you from sickness to health. A person who can help lead you in introspection to discover the roots and problems of why you are the way you are. If you grew up in a religious household, there is a strong possibility that what I am saying can seem taboo or even wrong. You were taught just to give it to God. When the problem and trauma happened to you when you were a kid, you were introduced to a pastor. I am sure with great intentions, they helped you as much as they did through prayer. You learned how to pray to be delivered from the pain but not heal the wound. Yet, even with that, I firmly believe it is wise to talk to Jesus and a professional specializing in these areas. You can be full of faith and still need a Life Coach. You can love the Lord with all of your heart and need a psychologist. You can be in ministry, leading a church, and still need a therapist. Getting the help you need isn't a lack of faith, and Jesus isn't mad at you; I firmly believe He is glad that you are doing so. I am a person of prayer and believe in prayer, but we as some Christians need to get better at giving adequate attention to the trauma that happens in a person's childhood and adult life that directly connects to their health and well-being. While you are praying and fasting, and while you are worshiping and interceding, you should be talking, confronting, and healing. How do you live, survive, and thrive after the altar call?

You may need a coach to help you break the stress and wounds passed down from generation to generation. Maybe, your parents modeled a lifestyle of coping instead of conquering. You had a refrigerator stock full of beer but a living room empty of conversations. Growing up, they experienced stress and trauma, but they spoke to a bottle and even bottled things up themselves. Thus, you assumed that you have to deal with it instead of heal from it. What if all these years you have been figuratively spraying air freshener in your life to get rid of the smell yet, failed to see what was in the trashcan? Overflowing from years of neglect is emotional, physical, and mental abuse. Beside it covered in mold is emotional, physical, and mental neglect. Throw out the trash, give attention to the root, and watch the flies die off and the smell dissipate. Please seek professional help, and they will help you learn how to not only survive but win.

**Breathe**

Have you ever hit a punching bag? One thing as a beginner you may notice is that you are holding your breath. Especially when you are trying to throw combos or a power punch, you can forget to breathe. Trying to punch harder but robbing yourself of the air to stay in the fight is a quick way to lose the capability to continue. I must admit when I started boxing; I would forget to breathe all the time. My coaches would yell, "breathe, Tim, breathe" during sparring. It wouldn't matter how many miles I ran to train and get in shape before the fight if I didn't breathe. As I was losing energy during training or sparring, my arms would start to drop, I was uncovered. The last thing I felt like doing was to throw another jab and keep my opponent at a distance. It's when knowledge and willpower went their separate ways because I had no energy to entertain them. I wonder if you have been fighting all these years but forgetting to breathe. I am a Life Coach myself and would love to walk with you to breakthrough and victory in your life; just reach out to me at www.TimothyMcCain.com. I am sorry if you have felt that you must do this all by yourself. I firmly believe that there is power in community, and maybe all this time, you needed someone in your life to remind you to breathe—a therapist to help you track down the roots of your issues that are presenting physical problems. We talked about both chemical imbalances and Trauma, which may be the birthing chambers of the depression you have been fighting. In the next few chapters, we will break down two other arenas, spiritual and circumstantial. You need to know that you are worth fighting for, so glove up, cover up, and get in the ring.

# CHAPTER 5

## SLIP

Honestly, out of all the chapters in this book, this is the one that I was the most concerned about writing. It is not because I am scared to talk about spiritual things but because it is in this arena that has been mismanaged by Christians the most. In this chapter, I will address depression and toxic, violent mental health from a spiritual angle. I am a spiritual person and a believer in Jesus and all that He has done for me. I am not "churchy," but I am saved. I am not religious, but I teach and preach and live the importance of having a relationship with God. I have spent well over a decade traveling worldwide, sharing hope and speaking to the real issues in the lives of families and individuals. I wrote my first book, "Crowns Are Greater Than Trophies" (yes, another shameless plug...go buy the book) after receiving many suicide letters while I was preaching around the nation. The letters all said similar things, such as, "If I kill myself, no one will miss me." Or "I have no friends, no one loves me." Sadly, many said, "I will try to tell my parents about my problems, and they will tell me to shut up and be quiet, until you have bills you don't have problems." So much of their pain was being unheard, yet they grew up in church and heard the Gospel preached every week. When I do extended camps, conferences, and services, I make sure that I address the pain, crisis, and trauma that the audience is going through. But I don't just say to give it to Jesus, but also to get help. It's ok to need Jesus in your life and even a therapist, life coach, and psychologist. I am happy to say that the ones that gave me the letters had an encounter that changed their lives, and they got the help they needed.

Depression and its ugly family members can walk through the doors of your life in many entrances. Thus far, you read about the chemical roots of depression as well as Crisis and Trauma. I want to be very clear that I am not saying that your depression is because the devil possesses you, and you are filled with demons. I feel that this single and sole approach towards mental health has been toxic and traumatizing for church attendees for decades. Thus, people in homes struggling with depression, anxiety, and other mental and emotional issues are scared to tell their parents because of what they know they may do to them. They will call the pastor, brought to the altar or front of the church, and people are going to lay hands and attempt to cast a spirit out. But my question is this; what if the root cause of the depression is not a spirit but rooted from a chemical imbalance? Of course, continue to pray, but pray for healing and get the help to get healed, not merely just deliverance.

I wish I could sit down and meet every person that is reading this book and hear your story and what you believe. Maybe you are a spiritual person, and these kinds of things make sense to you. Or possibly, you are not a spiritual or religious person and what I am talking about is the same as a fairytale to you. Regardless of where you stand, I hope that this chapter confirms the spiritual side of things or informs you that one exists.

*1 Peter 5:8 NIV*

*"Be alert and of sober mind. Your enemy the devil prowls around like a roaring lion looking for someone to devour."*

A roaming lion is looking for a moment of opportunity to pounce on its prey and consume them. The devil isn't much different as he searches for and capitalizes on moments, pain, and areas unhealed to bring pain and destruction. In areas of unforgiveness, he will sit on and fester a cycle of pain, and you rehearse the trauma over and over. He looks for the time you make a mistake and ushers guilt and condemnation, so you never look for help because you believe you deserve to be there in the first place. Christians are quick to blame the devil for anything that happens in their lives in a negative way. Shouting from the top of their voices that they are taking back everything the devil stole from them. But what if it was never something that was stolen, but given away? What if the devil never trespassed in your household, family, and mental health but was invited? What if the infestation accrued through an invitation?

**Play Dough**

I don't believe that every person struggling with depression is possessed by the devil's demons. For some Christians, that statement alone would be considered to be heresy, but it is not. It is easier to blame the devil for the state of our lives than to look in the mirror. It is easier to preach a sermon about the devil than to examine our own behaviors. So many stand on a soapbox and proclaim that "the devil made me do it," but if that was the case, then you are possessed. I believe that possession is real but do I think that every person that makes that statement is? Of course not. The devil didn't make you do it; you were influenced, and your sinful nature longed for it. The devil did not possess Adam and Eve, and even after eating the forbidden fruit, they pointed fingers at the devil and each other, saying, so and so made me do it, or its such and such fault. For many people, it is not a question of possession but oppression. My son loves to play with play dough, which is one of our favorite pastimes to do together. If you take playdough in your hands and squeeze it, then let go, you can see oppression right before your eyes. The dough's indentions occurred because it was squeezed from the outside, not pulled out from the inside. It is in this arena that many people find themselves, the place of squeezing.

Do you feel like you are in the enemy's hands and pressed on all ends? Do you think that your depression, anxiety, and deep sadness are always at the forefront of your mind? Do you believe that it is your fault that you are the way you are because of your mistakes? Are you not seeking help because you believe that you deserve to live in darkness and feel abandoned? Have you placed your identity in your affliction and don't know who you are without it? Is the enemy capitalizing on your pain, trauma, and crisis? Please entertain this thought for a moment; what if your freedom occurs from, again assuming that it birthed solely from a spiritual place, isn't casting it out but crucifying it? By this statement, I mean that your oppression may be rooted in your "flesh" and sinful nature and not a spirit hovering over your life at every waking moment. The Bible uses the word flesh to talk about the primal, sinful, and inherent nature that every person obtains.

Genesis 3:1-13 NIV

*3 Now the serpent was more crafty than any of the wild animals the Lord God had made. He said to the woman, "Did God really say, 'You must not eat from any tree in the garden'?" 2 The woman said to the serpent, "We may eat fruit from the trees in the garden, 3 but God did say, 'You must not eat fruit from the tree that is in the middle of the garden, and you must not touch it, or you will die.'" 4 "You will not certainly die," the serpent said to the woman. 5 "For*

*God knows that when you eat from it your eyes will be opened, and you will be like God, knowing good and evil." 6 When the woman saw that the fruit of the tree was good for food and pleasing to the eye, and also desirable for gaining wisdom, she took some and ate it. She also gave some to her husband, who was with her, and he ate it. 7 Then the eyes of both of them were opened, and they realized they were naked; so they sewed fig leaves together and made coverings for themselves. 8 Then the man and his wife heard the sound of the Lord God as he was walking in the garden in the cool of the day, and they hid from the Lord God among the trees of the garden. 9 But the Lord God called to the man, "Where are you?" 10 He answered, "I heard you in the garden, and I was afraid because I was naked; so I hid." 11 And he said, "Who told you that you were naked? Have you eaten from the tree that I commanded you not to eat from?" 12 The man said, "The woman you put here with me—she gave me some fruit from the tree, and I ate it." 13 Then the Lord God said to the woman, "What is this you have done?" The woman said, "The serpent deceived me, and I ate."*

The serpent used crafty words to manipulate Adam and Eve to eat the fruit. In the book of Genesis, it is sharing how he said, "Did God really say." These words helped usher her along to the compromise as many for the first time questioned their truth. The devil didn't force-feed them; they chose to eat; why? Because after that conversation, they saw that it was "good and pleasing to the eye." They engaged in something that they knew was wrong thus suffered emotional trauma that stuck with them. They not only saw themselves through a different lens but each other.

1 Corinthians 9:27 NKJV

"But I discipline my body and bring *it* into subjection, lest, when I have preached to others, I myself should become disqualified."

Have you been fighting oppressive depression, worry, and anxiety due to the choices you have made? The first step of victory is to know that you are in a fight in the first place. Are you aware that your fight's root cause may be due to an opponent you have created, welcomed, and entertained? We can't cast out our flesh or rebuke it in Jesus' name; we must crucify it daily and with focused intentions. I am not saying to crucify your body literally but to be intentional to see the toxic habits and characteristics we have and attempt to stop them. If you have allowed your addiction to alcohol to destroy your family, end your marriage, and wreck your life, you aren't going to rebuke the devil and keep drinking. No, you are going to stop drinking, get healthy, confront your behaviors, and fight for redemption. Maybe you noticed that you had broken relationships all around you, and your belief is that the devil is the sole reason for the attacks in your household. Again, not removing the enemy from the equation, but maybe it is the vile gossiping tongue that you have that is causing division and separation. What if the devil in your life doesn't have a pitchfork but a computer. You feel like you don't have any community and that no one likes you on social media, but you are a troll causing strife with strangers and commenting on a post that doesn't even obtain to you. You are lonely and depressed because you can't find a good man or woman, but you treat them like garbage only then to say that all men are dogs and women are nothing "golddiggas." Do you get the point yet? It is a great error to assume that we feel the way we feel because the devil is always causing it when he is just capitalizing on it. Stop looking down toward hell to see the problem and take a look in the mirror. How do you spiritually uproot and shut the door of depression deriving from an oppressive spiritual root? Walk-in your authority as a believer, give it to Jesus and allow Him to strengthen you to fight your fight of faith. The role of the Holy Spirit isn't simply designated for your Sunday morning experiences but for everyday life. God empowers us to stop toxic actions that are holding the door open for restrictions and acidic behaviors. If your mental state is a byproduct of your actions, it only makes sense to evaluate your actions. All the enemy is looking for is a chance, not an invitation. He isn't looking for the red carpet to be rolled out with his name in lights, but a crack window of opportunity called neglect and compromise. Search your heart and ask God for wisdom and enlightenment about the state of your spiritual life. Could it be that the flies flying all around your mind and the crappy actions from your life are the enticing and intoxicating smell ushering them in? As you spend the time swatting all the flies, shut the entrances, cracks, and openings.

## Puppet Strings

Yet, even with that said, demonic possession is still a very real thing, as we can read in scripture. To be clear and to sound like a broken record, I am not saying that possession is fake or the devil isn't real. I simply believe that it is an error to jump the gun to stand on the notion that your situation is happening because the devil made you do it. It is easy to believe this because it doesn't require us to take responsibility for our own actions. But once again, this is all smoke and mirrors because we should still ponder how the possession happened in the first place. Mark chapter 5 talks about a man possessed by demons in such a way that it strongly affected his mental health and physical wellbeing.

*Mark 5:1-20*

*5 They went across the lake to the region of the Gerasenesa. 2 When Jesus got out of the boat, a man with an impure spirit came from the tombs to meet him. 3 This man lived in the tombs, and no one could bind him anymore, not even with a chain. 4 For he had often been chained hand and foot, but he tore the chains apart and broke the irons on his feet. No one was strong enough to subdue him. 5 Night and day among the tombs and in the hills he would cry out and cut himself with stones.*

*6 When he saw Jesus from a distance, he ran and fell on his knees in front of him. 7 He shouted at the top of his voice, "What do you want with me, Jesus, Son of the Most High God? In God's name don't torture me!" 8 For Jesus had said to him, "Come out of this man, you impure spirit!" 9 Then Jesus asked him, "What is your name?" "My name is Legion," he replied, "for we are many." 10 And he begged Jesus again and again not to send them out of the area. 11 A large herd of pigs was feeding on the nearby hillside. 12 The demons begged Jesus, "Send us among the pigs; allow us to go into them." 13 He gave them permission, and the impure spirits came out and went into the pigs. The herd, about two thousand in number, rushed down the steep bank into the lake and were drowned.*

*14 Those tending the pigs ran off and reported this in the town and countryside, and the people went out to see what had happened.15 When they came to Jesus, they saw the man who had been possessed by the legion of demons, sitting there, dressed and in his right mind; and they were afraid. 16 Those who had seen it told the people what had happened to the demon-possessed man—and told about the pigs as well. 17 Then the people began to plead with Jesus to leave their region. 18 As Jesus was getting into the boat, the man who had been demon-possessed begged to go with him. 19 Jesus did not let him, but said, "Go home to your own people and tell them how much the Lord has done for you, and how he has had mercy on you." 20 So the man went away and began to tell in the Decapolis how much Jesus had done for him. And all the people were amazed.*

Mark doesn't give us much background information about the man possessed by the legion of demons. I can only make assumptions using extra-biblical studies, the culture of the time, and context clues. But one thing is for sure: this man was controlled by demonic spirits and affected his mental, physical health, and overall life. He exercised self-harm when he took sharp rocks and cut himself. Once again, I believe it is important to pause and state that I am not saying that if you cut yourself, you are demon-possessed. However, talking about oppression and what the enemy of your soul desires to capitalize upon is for you to harm yourself. Do you know what it is like to not to want to live anymore? Maybe you have entertained thoughts of dying, so you don't have to fight another day. Deep and dark depression will lead you to a dark place with a slippery slope.

Typically, in many Christian circles, if someone found out that a person was cutting or self-harming, the only things done are prayer and deliverance. What needs to be done is to take steps after the prayer and give pain and hurt over to Jesus but get to the issues' roots. Learning how to process and talk about your pain so you don't internalize it is crucial. Learn how to get to a place that don't see a blade on your arm as a point of release but discover a safe and productive place to release. These matters must be addressed on all ends and not solely in the spiritual plane. Prayer should be and is a place that you can process emotions and feelings, but maybe you have been told "just pray about it," and it never fixes anything. If you think that prayer is just you talking out loud to a God that doesn't speak back, you are mistaken. The easiest way I can explain prayer is a therapy session with God. His office is always open, and He always answers His phone. He doesn't charge you a price because He already paid it. Prayer is where you share what is on your heart and mind, and an exchange occurs. If there were confusion, you would gain wisdom, maybe there was fear, but there will be an exchange of faith. Having a prayer life is having an encounter with Jesus and transformative things happen.

1 Peter 5:7

"Cast all your anxiety on him because he cares for you."

After the man's encounter with Jesus, it left him freed and restored. He was dressed and in his right mind. It was as if he was a completely different person and the people in the region witnessed that very thing. He no longer lived in a tomb in isolation, harming himself but moved publicly, sharing this story of freedom and deliverance. In this man's cause, he didn't need a therapist, life coach, or psychologist; he needed a savior, an encounter with God. He got his mind back, his peace and wellbeing. Maybe you know what it is like to live in darkness and confusion. Maybe you have a first-hand witness of the devil trying to rob, kill, and destroy you. You know what it is like to be bombarded with lies that repeat detrimental words that impede your ability to live free and whole. You have tried talking about your problems; you even tried therapy. I would encourage you to continue to do all of those things, but don't overlook how oppression is a real thing that needs a real God to step in. I firmly believe that some problems have spiritual roots that require spiritual solutions. I pray that every demonic stronghold and influence in your life is broken in the name of Jesus.

## Priceless

As I stated at the beginning of this chapter, is that out of all the chapters in this book, this is the one I was the most hesitant to write. It's like when someone places an extremely valuable, priceless, fragile item in your hands, and all you can think about is protecting it and not dropping it. <u>The hesitation is from the awareness of its worth, not the ignorance of its importance.</u> I don't know who is going to read this book. I don't know if you believe that Jesus even existed or you think He is a fictional character. I don't know if you are like a spirit-filled Jedi, and you feel like you are close to the heart of God already, and you attempt to fix all issues of life in your prayer room. For the one who is unaware of the spiritual realm and how some things are based on spiritual roots and attacks, you will be equipped to fight back. The person who speaks in tongues about their problems in their prayer room will also need to know that you also have to seek physical and practical actions. To be spiritually minded doesn't mean you have to be presently disconnected and unaware. I have pastored for years, and I have had encounters and conversations with people that make me shake my head to this day. I have lost count of how many times a parent called my office about their teenager because they think demons or the devil possesses them or is attacking them. So they come into my office, and I spend some time listening and talking. Many times it has nothing to do with spiritual things at all but personalities and communication skills. Many times, extroverted parents think that something is wrong with their introverted kid because all their other kids aren't like them. They don't speak much and spend time alone with themselves; thus, they assume the devil is bringing depression on them. As an introvert myself, I have to tell them that that may not be the case, and just because they recharge and thrive by themselves doesn't mean they are depressed and lonely. In those moments, the mistake is to bypass asking questions and only bring out my anointing oil and pray against a demon that isn't there, but it is just them creating more trauma. They grow up in an environment where loving parents are unaware and call them a demon and don't believe them when they tell them that nothing is wrong. Thus, it erodes the line of communication to which they think that talking to their parents is pointless because they don't listen.

## Red Cup

Years ago, there was an uproar in the Christian community about a red Starbucks cup. It didn't have Merry Christmas on it, and thus some people took deep offense over it and thought it was an attack against their faith and trying to take Christ out of Christmas. I'm going to be frank with you, it was embarrassing. 100% disappointing seeing how some Christians were vocal about a red cup and silent about so many other issues that really matter. First of all, it is a red cup; second of all, Starbucks is not a church or a Christian organization, so why are Christians holding non-Christian places to church standards? It was not a moral issue; that was a church culture issue that Christians attempted to add spiritual importance. This was a public platform to witness how some things aren't resolved spiritually. This is not to throw out spiritual things and to believe that it isn't essential because it is vital to understand. We can't pray at things that we need to learn how to think through. God has given us both the spirit and the brain, and we need to know how to use both.

## SLIP

In boxing, there is a term called slipping. When someone throws a punch, you move your head out of the way but in a position to counter. A slip isn't running away from the fight but avoiding a punch to stay in the fight. With great footwork and a boxing IQ, you can slip and position yourself to attack. When you are slipping, you have to keep your eye on your opponent. Boxers will tell you that it is tiring when you throw punches, and they aren't landing.

It is time that you learn how to slip from the enemy of your soul attack. Wear him out and drain his energy by making him miss the attempts to bring harm or pain in your life. Search your life for the doors of opportunities that you may have left open for him to come in and cause destruction. Slip away from the toxic relationships in your life that are pulling you in the wrong directions. Slip out of the self-medicating actions that you have started to help you make it through life. The drugs, drinking, cutting, and toxic relationship with food isn't helping you; it's harming you. Slip and strike every time his lies are thrown at you. Slip the lie that you aren't going to make it and strike with the fact that you can do all things through Christ that gives you strength. Slip the lie that you are hopeless and strike back, knowing that God is fighting for you, and you are going to start fighting for yourself. Slip the lie that you will always be depressed and strike with a prayer life, a life coach, therapist, psychologist, or whoever you need in your corner.

I am not saying to Cover up and just take the punches. Maybe you have seen it in boxing when someone is on the ropes, and they lift their forearms to their face and slightly crouch at the waist to protect themselves. They are just standing there getting hit and just trying to survive while protecting themselves as much as possible. Don't just spend your time Covering up but slip. You don't have to stand there and take a beating in your mental and emotional health but fight back by fighting for yourself.

# CHAPTER 6

## HAND WRAP

There are moments in your life that happen that knock you off your feet. At the writing of this exact chapter, I got the news that my father was in the hospital with possible kidney issues or even failure. I write about his influence and impact in my life in my book, "This Is Your Chance." He had a work ethic that was amazing and instilled it in his children. He was never rich with money, but he was wealthy with compassion and a desire to help anyone in need. I will go into more detail later in this book, but he suffered three strokes a couple of years ago that turned his life upside down. Frankly, it does seem that "when it rains, it pours."

To make matters worse, in this circumstance, I can't drive up to North Carolina to see him due to the recent shutdown and CDC guidelines. For reference, it is currently the year 2020 at the time that I am writing this book. The year 2020 will forever be a year in history that generations will read about and study. So many traumatic events have occurred every single month throughout the year. COVID-19 has killed hundreds of thousands at the time of writing this book. People have lost their businesses to things outside of their control. There are uproars for injustices all around the nation. In addition, people are dying alone in hospitals away from family and friends due to COVID-19. Families that never knew what a financial struggle was before were now fighting through it for the first time. Where they were once loose with cash now had a hard time obtaining it. Jobs closing left and right, leaving people unable to pay their rent, forcing them to get evicted and homeless. For the first time for many people, they encountered a firm grip of depression. They were feeling hopeless and broken without any light at the end of a tunnel. There is a great chance that you may be someone that doesn't have clinical depression. Maybe your deep sadness and anxiety aren't due to chemical imbalances in your body. In moments of deep sadness and depression everyone is at risk to encounter circumstantial depression.

This is a state of depression that didn't come from a demonic spiritual attack over their lives. There wasn't a sudden chemical imbalance that they confronted within themselves. It didn't emerge from the sudden realization of childhood trauma and crisis. The hardships of life were a tidal wave that crushed the shores of people's homes and lives without emotionally preparing. When I teach or life coach, I tell my clients that there is a difference between "life happening to you" and "you happening to life." When it's "you happening to life," you can make sense of the situation because it could be traced to the consequence of your actions. It is hard to work through nonetheless, but at least you can wrap your head around the situation. But when it is a moment that it is "life happening to you," it is hard to process because so much of it is outside of your control. These are the moments when life seems to be flat out unfair. These are the crisis that occurs in the traffic of life, leaving us broken down on the side of the road. Depression, deep sadness, anxiety, worry, and other emotions eat away at your stability like termites thrive in moments of uncertainty. Traditionally you can keep your depression under control because you find areas that you can control. But in these moments, you feel like all your peace in life is slipping through your fingers, and you become undone at the seams of your understanding.

Chemical, Crisis and Trauma, and spiritually are the areas of depression addressed thus far in this book. I am sure that there are some of you that fall into those categories. When it comes to depression stemmed from the hard circumstances of life, it becomes an equal opportunist. It is vital in these moments of life that you focus on your self-care.

There is a man named Elijah that had his life rocked to the core when a crisis in his life derived from a significant circumstance. The story is remarkable because we get to see God's interaction with this man of God filled with worry. God's interaction with Elijah is taboo for some religious people because God didn't respond to him with a rebuke, anger, or disapproval; he didn't beat him or told him to get a switch from the tree. He didn't reach for his majestic belt, put on a stern face, and raise His voice. God didn't tell him that He didn't have enough faith or call him names. He didn't give him a sermon, lecture, or a ted talk. In fact, God didn't rebuke a demon or devil or call out sin. God the father, fathered Elijah through His pain and suffering. It is easy to forget that God is a father and not just some deity in heaven far away from us. In fact, it is quite the opposite. He is a father that spends time with us and helps us through our struggles and problems. What God was teaching Elijah at this moment was so profound and yet extremely simple.

Nonetheless, even though it was simple in theory, it is overwhelmingly hard to apply. What life lesson am I referring to? It is self-care.

*1 Kings 19:1-9*

*"Now Ahab told Jezebel everything Elijah had done and how he had killed all the prophets with the sword. 2 So Jezebel sent a messenger to Elijah to say, "May the gods deal with me, be it ever so severely, if by this time tomorrow I do not make your life like that of one of them." 3 Elijah was afraid and ran for his life. When he came to Beersheba in Judah, he left his servant there, 4 while he himself went a day's journey into the wilderness. He came to a broom bush,*

*sat down under it and prayed that he might die. "I have had enough, Lord," he said. "Take my life; I am no better than my ancestors." 5 Then he lay down under the bush and fell asleep. All at once an angel touched him and said, "Get up and eat." 6 He looked around, and there by his head was some bread baked over hot coals, and a jar of water. He ate and drank and then lay down again. 7 The angel of the Lord came back a second time and touched him and said, "Get up and eat, for the journey is too much for you." 8 So he got up and ate and drank. Strengthened by that food, he traveled forty days and forty nights until he reached Horeb, the mountain of God. 9 There he went into a cave and spent the night."*

Elijah experienced an emotional roller coaster that shook him to the core of his being and belief. Right before Jezebel threatened his life, he just did a showdown with people known as the prophets of Baal. Elijah and the prophets agreed on a test for their god to rain down fire from the heavens to prove who served the true real god. Elijah, filled with confidence, let the prophets go first as they cried out, but nothing happened. He even started to ridicule them and "talk junk" when nothing was happening for them. He said (paraphrasing) that maybe your god is out relieving himself (using the restroom), that is why he isn't responding. Almost coming across as cocky, he told them to take the bull sacrifice and pour buckets of water on it. With the sacrifice drenched with water, he called out to God, knowing without a doubt that He heard him, and fire came down from heaven and consumed the sacrifice. Elijah was in an emotionally high place, but the circumstances around him were about to change drastically; as you read, when he heard the news from Jezebel, his tune quickly changed from his mountaintop experience to the darkness that greeted him in the valley of his uncertainty. He was experiencing a level of deep sadness or depression that swung his emotional pendulum from certainty to unrelenting anxiety, worry, and fear. It is important to see the progression in his life in this area as it was a gradual speed ramp that we can see take place verse to verse. After hearing the news, one of the first things he did was self-isolation and that my friends can be dangerous.

**Self-Isolation**

*3 Elijah was afraid and ran for his life. When he came to Beersheba in Judah, **he left his servant there, 4 while he himself** went a day's journey into the wilderness. He came to a broom bush, sat down under it and prayed **that he might die. "I have had enough, Lord,"** he said. **"Take my life;** I am no better than my ancestors."*

The first thing Elijah did was to remove himself from the company around him to be by himself. He left his servant and helper and isolated himself into the wilderness in an emotional state of panic and worry. I wish Elijah shared in more detail about all that was going on in his mind. It is important that we remember that Elijah and all characters of the bible were real people who went through real things with real emotions. Take a moment and place yourself in his shoes; how does it feel? I assume that the experience doesn't feel foreign but normal. You know what it is like to get into a depressing state and to pull away from the community around you. Maybe you stop answering your phone calls and ignore your text messages because you don't want to talk to anyone. Now you are alone physically but bombarded with negative thoughts that come in and out without a sense of control, wreaking havoc on your mental health. The deep bottomless pit you feel at the base of your stomach that sends a sensation to your mind reminds you of the assumed hollow existence of your life. Like trying to grab a wet bar of soap with latex gloves, the notion of peace of mind that you reach for is seemingly impossible to hold on to.  You willingly removed yourself from people and created your own environment that cycles your negative thought life, in which you don't have anyone to shake you free from it. Elijah had his wilderness and environment, but what it yours? His was a place he went to and through but, is yours one you create when you are in this emotional state? Do you listen to depressing music, turn off the lights, and grab the action or substance of choice, so you don't have to feel your feelings?

In his dark moment, he cried out to God to take his life because he is overwhelmed by all that is happening. Maybe you haven't said Elijah's exact words, but perhaps you have in that dark place wished that you would be removed from existence. In the heat of the moment, the thought of not living seems alluring because you won't have to face the pain and fear. Have you ever been tired of being tired? Deep sadness, crippling depression, overwhelming anxiety, and unrelenting worry is a four-headed hydra with an appetite for your health and wellbeing. At the same time, you are trying to confront one issue and cut off its head, only to face the others while the severed head regrows in the background more deadly than before. Its venom paralyzes hope, dismantles courage, and like a python, suffocates faith. Elijah felt abandoned, forgotten, confused, and alone. His fear-induced depression, anxiety, worry, and sadness changed their address and attempted to make their residence in his mind to stay. Yet, what happens next is remarkable for many reasons. God sent an angel to tend to him in one of the darkest and lowest moments of his life. A genuine and authentic ministry display was about to occur in the most trying season in his life. It is important to see what didn't happen at this moment. I am by no means saying that these actions are not important or needed at times, but it is important that we know the times that it is needed. But what didn't happen was God giving him a lecture, sermon, or a PowerPoint presentation rebuking his actions and calling out his faith. God didn't call him out for hurting and emotional bleeding out from the crisis he is facing. God didn't call him a "snowflake" or saying he had a victim mentality for being honest about his pain and living in his truth. What happened next can be so simple that it can be perceived as unnecessary, yet it was profoundly important. The angel instructed him to go to sleep, drink, and eat some food. At this moment, it wasn't prayer, fasting, or warfare. It didn't require speaking in tongues, calling on the church's elders, and casting out demons. In this occurrence, it wasn't shouting out scriptures or saying the Lord's model prayer or some other religious activity. Not to say that spirituality isn't important; however, at this moment, what was needed for Elijah to recover was rest and recovery. It was a crash course of learning how vital self-care truly is and how crucial it is to know and prioritize.

*"5 Then he lay down under the bush and fell asleep. All at once an angel touched him and said, "Get up and eat." 6 He looked around, and there by his head was some bread baked over hot coals, and a jar of water. He ate and drank and then lay down again. 7 The angel of the Lord came back a second time and touched him and said, "Get up and eat, for the journey is too much for you." 8 So he got up and ate and drank. Strengthened by that food, he traveled forty days and forty nights until he reached Horeb, the mountain of God. 9 There he went into a cave and spent the night."*

## Breakfast In Bed

Sometimes one of the most important things you can do is take a nap. Elijah's stress levels were through the roof. His mind has been racing, creating possible scenarios that didn't happen or what could happen. When we sleep at night, it allows our sympathetic nervous system to recover. This is needed because it is a part of the body that controls our fight or flight response. Elijah's sympathetic nervous system was working overtime and needed some rest and recovery. How can the most simple tasks that our bodies long for often become the last things we give it? I find it remarkable that God created humankind with the means to fight, strive, and overcome, to rest, and recover so the fight can continue. When was the last time you rested? How have you prioritized your sleep? Maybe you don't give it much thought; thus, you pump your body with caffeine to keep it up when it is begging for a moment for your mind to recover?

In addition to sleep, the angel woke him up from his sleep and provided food for him to eat. Yes, food! It was Heaven's Uber Eats that arrived right on time. God was attentive to Elijah's physical health and wellbeing. He didn't ask him, but encouraged him to do just that. Depression can reveal itself in our lives in many ways. When they feel in the slumps due to mental battles, the last thing they want to do is eat. They lose their appetite; this is not to overlook how others swing on the other end of self-mediating their feeling with overindulgence. The angel gave him bread, which is carbohydrates and water. Carbs are important for our body to consume because they turn into glycogen, which our bodies use as energy. Many studies point to how a lack of carbs could trigger anxiety and depression as it affects a person's drop in mood. In addition to the bread and sleep, he was given water to consume and recover. Once again, studies are showing how dehydration can trigger anxiety and other issues connected to our mental health. I strongly encourage you to take time out of your day and study the effects of food and drink on your mental health. What if you are trying to fight this battle but not giving your body what it is asking for to win the fight in the first place?

Twice the angel of the LORD woke him up from his sleep and told him to get something to eat. Not a single time in these interactions was spiritual warfare mentioned. Not a single time was God mad at him because he was honest about how he felt and what he was going through. Not a single time was he told to suck it up and be a man. Not a single time was he told that he wasn't a man of God because he was feeling his feelings. His faith wasn't questioned because he was struggling; in fact, the angel of the Lord acknowledged the stress of his fight " the journey has been too much for you." I will address this in an upcoming chapter, but "church folk" have been dying in the pews of their sanctuary because they aren't honest with what is going on in their lives. "Give it to God" doesn't mean you are freed from personal effort and responsibilities to ensure you are doing what He needs you to do for your victory. Preachers and Pastors are yelling in error from pulpits that if you say how you feel, then you don't have faith, or if you are concerned about it is a lack of faith. Thus, people are taught to fake it till they make it, but they can't make it any longer. It is vital to be honest with the state of your life, so your healing can start to take place. A great place to be honest with yourself is how you are treating your body. Is your lack of good rest feeding that tapeworm of depression that grows while you are withering away? **The bottom line**

**is we can't heal what we conceal, and we can't mend what we refuse to confront.** God being the heavenly father that He is, showed and modeled compassion and the importance of self-care. Once Elijah was "strengthened by the food," as verse 8 states, he was in a better place mentally, emotionally, physically, and spiritually to take the journey. Elijah would later have another encounter where he hears God's still quiet voice in the following verses. Yet, it is amazing to me to process the idea that Elijah heard and listened to the gentle whisper of God's voice after anxiety's mantic voice was silenced after his recovery.

### Self-care Isn't Selfish

Every single person that is walking this earth has circumstances in their lives that can cause unrelenting stress. It strives to become an impact drill that drives the nails of stress in with consistent force, staking our attention to the problems at hand. It glues us to the seat of the plays of our life as it showcases an Oscar-winning performance of the dilemmas acted out in repeated fashion, giving alternate endings, which none displays you as the winner. Every waking moment and even while you dream, depression, anxiety, worry, and deep sadness takes the stage to bow as fear gives them a standing ovation, demanding an encore where they happily oblige. You want to muster up the willpower to fight back, and, like Showtime The Apollo, take the hook and yank them off the stage of your attention. Elijah's attention to his self-care helped him step out of the cave of his circumstantial depression. He was visited by the angel that had his best interest in mind that acknowledged his situation. Like a therapist, the angel of the LORD helped him work through this dark moment of his life.

Depression can thrive in Chemical imbalances, induced Trauma, Spiritual attack, Circumstantial crisis, or many other areas. Maybe you are fighting through the circumstances of your life that are trying to bully you and shove you in the locker of depression. Keep fighting forward, give attention to your physical and mental health, and give yourself a fighting chance. It would love nothing more than to take your willpower away and for you to believe a lie that your efforts are worthless. The bottom line is this; your self-care isn't a selfish action but vital to prioritize. Eat well, sleep well, find a stress relieving based hobby, and do the thing that makes you unwind and happy. Seek a therapist and a life coach that can help you work through the circumstances in your life. Warning: here comes another shameless plug, but hire me and let me help you fight through the storms of your life.

### Wrap Your Hands

Under the hands of every boxer should be a proper hand wrap—this simple discipline helps protect the fighter from injuries to their hands and wrist. It doesn't take much time to do before you put on your gloves, but you will be amazed at how many people overlook this step because they think they don't need it. But eventually, after repeated punches, it brings wear and tears to the wrist, affecting the punch and for others completely removes them from the sport altogether. It is protection that is covered up that many in public can't see but is paramount to success. Using hand wraps is a boxer's act of self-care and self-love. It can be tedious and not very glamorous to stand in front of your heavy bag and take the time to be attentive to the details, but something that must not be overlooked. Once again, easier said than done, like when depression is overwhelming. The simple task such as eating and taking a shower can seem exhausting. Yet, with every fighter, a coach helps them do what they, at that moment, don't feel like doing. He or she can remind you to wrap your hands, or the therapist can aid you with introspection to health and recovery. The circumstances of your life are calling you out to fight whether you are ready or not. The punches are coming even if you didn't train for it or prepare. Stop telling yourself that you don't have the time to take care of yourself and strive to make time. Wrap your hands and train hard because you can win, whether you are in a fight now or prepare for the ones coming.

# CHAPTER 7

# ROAD WORK

There is not enough honesty in the world, and when someone is expressive about their feelings, they are attacked and told to stop complaining. Thus, many people are dying knowing they need help yet not knowing where to go and who to go to. Depression in the Christian community has been considered synonymous with a demonic attack that they rebuke the spirit but ignore the mind and heart's health. The place that is supposed to be the sanctuary then becomes a stage where people act out perfection while under the mask, are rotting, hiding behind the false narrative of "hold fast the confession of your tongue" because if you talk about it, you will give power to it. Many issues, including depression, fester behind praise dances, inspirational sermons, tithe and offerings, mission trips, and much more. In many Christian circles, they are not taught to talk about their problems; they just pray about them. Once again, I am a person of prayer and believe in it, but we must stop using God as our excuse not to confront our feelings instead of Him being our refuge that is the safe place to do it.

I wrote this book because I am frustrated, disappointed, and tired of seeing people crumble under the weight of depression, deep sadness, and anxiety, only to hear others say, "just smile" or "don't think about it." Depression is an ugly monster whose claws are long, and fangs are sharp, hunting in isolation even while you are surrounded by crowds of people, yet still feeling alone. You must learn to be open about what you are facing and get the help you need. But where do you go? Who do you tell? Where can you feel safe knowing that you won't be judged but helped when you express how you feel? Maybe these are some of the many questions you ponder, that cycles in your mind, that you used to write your permission slip to stay quiet. You keep telling yourself that you will figure it out alone. You wake up in the morning and give yourself a pep talk just to make it out of the house. You get in the parking lot of your place of work only to look in the rearview mirror to tell yourself that you can make it. Figuratively, painting on a smile on your tired soul, striving to continue day by day. How do I know all of these things? Because I live through them every day. These last few years have been the most difficult years of my entire life. It has been circumstances after circumstances in labor, birthing children of hardship repeatedly for years. Once I fight through one problem or crisis, another one appears out of nowhere. But where do strong people go to be weak, and when can you have those moments to be vulnerable without people taking advantage of you. I'm tired of the "call me if you need anything" or the "how are you doing" being simple pleasantries and not genuine extensions of aid or concern. I hate that "I'm praying for you" from the Christian community has become a default response rather than a daily mission. I have been preaching and in ministry for well over a decade nonstop and gave my entire life over the call. My back used to be an empty canvas void of wounds now covered with scars and fresh cuts from repeated backstabs through the years. I wanted to quit the ministry more times than I can count, then, without fail, I have an encounter helping someone out of their crisis that reminds me why I do the things I do. I can't say that I have walked through these years unscathed from the letdown of "friends" coming in and out taking more than they deposit. I made up in my mind that I will no longer chase after "spiritual fathers" only to wind up neglected, forgotten, and worse off. Instead of chasing after or looking for spiritual fathers of the faith, I determined that I will just strive to become one (don't get me wrong, I have also had plenty of great voices and relationships through the years). Why am I telling you this and being open about my feelings? Because I will not ask you to do something that I am not willing to do myself. I have had to fight through all these feelings and more while preaching to the masses and leading ministries. I know without a doubt that the fight of anxiety, depression, deep sadness, and other issues along these lines plague the mind of ministers, pastors, and leaders all around the nation. You will never know because the moment they are open about what they are combating, there is a chance that the Christian community will grab figurative tiki torches and riot against them and all they are fighting to do. They can't be open because the platform has been mutated into a pedestal intentionally, or unintentionally, where they don't have permission to be human. At the same time, people forget that they are striving to be Christ-LIKE; they aren't Christ.

There is something called smiling depression. You can be depressed, smile, and even make other people smile and laugh, and I totally think there's also something that we should coin as preaching depression. A Pastor or minister could preach fire everywhere to everybody and still be depressed. Preaching hope to others yet still feel hopeless and preaching courage to others and still feel fearful. They can preach the truth and still be fighting lies. Even with this statement, the problem is that someone read it and thinks that the minister or pastor is feeling this way because they are in sin or don't have enough of God, or aren't praying hard enough. And it's sad that religious cultures equate human experiences and mental health that are directly connected to someone's length of prayer time. During biblical times, religious people equated a person's sickness due to a sin, which isn't true. These beliefs aren't far from many ways of thinking; some people still entertain them today.

When we have missed managed prayer, it can become a session that we give to God, "let go and let God" as people say. However, these words or actions don't relinquish us from responsibilities, yet in error; we can let it become another coping mechanism that we use to not confront the matters at hand. The same way that we can use the excuse, "waiting on God" as the scapegoat to allow our procrastination to lead us when we have already been guided about what to do. There is power in prayer and intercession. There is freedom when we allow God to lead, guide us, and intervene in our lives. However, the issue occurs when we forget that faith without works is dead. If I give it to God, then I don't have to think about it; if I give it to God, I don't have to talk about it; if I give it to God, I don't have to process the issue. If I give it to God, I don't have to talk about the molestation; if I give it to God, I don't have to talk about the divorce; if I give it to God, I don't have to talk about the problems. When, in fact, our God is our counselor, our teacher, our healer, our doctor who specializes in our entire existence. But what doctor or counselor heals without surgery, and how can you have surgery without attention? How can you have a mending without a cutting to get to the roots?

Religion is a drug, coping mechanism, and every Sunday, self-medicating action. Don't ever get it confused with having a relationship with Jesus. Because Jesus walks with you through your Valley to heal religion, which just wants you to shout at it, not fight through it.

## Frustration

I had to choose what I am going to do with my frustrations. I told myself that I have two options; I can let it consume me or capitalize on it to fuel and push me. The same fire that consumes homes and burns forest fields is the same force under rockets pushing it onto space. The difference is its placements, control, and intentions. A wild forest fire simply spreads and burns everything it touches. It burns bridges, relationships, and things held dear because of its raw passion, pain, and blinding power. But that raw passion, pain, and energy under a rocket used with control can launch it into space and different atmospheres. The channeled frustrations create the escape velocity thrusting it out of the gravity pulling it down to orbit the issues. When it harnesses our frustration in its raw form, it can become an ore used to create something powerful. Like a blacksmith crafting tools and weapons in the heat, pressing and crushing steel, it hammers frustration into a useful tool known as purpose.

I refuse to waste a scar, a fight, or a journey. I didn't go through all the hell these last few years for no reason. My purpose has been revealed with greater clarity than ever before, and this book is part of it. You need to know that you aren't alone, and that other people are fighting battles in private just like you. You need to know that you aren't God's exception for issues that are too great for Him to work out, or problems too massive for His intervention. You need to know that it is ok to hurt, feel your feelings, and seek the help you need. In the previous few chapters, I introduced to you four categories where depression can be birthed. If you stand in any of those places or just read this book to help someone, be aware that your transparency and honesty are vital. These next few pages are raw, open, and a detailed account of my journey in the last few years. I don't want to ask you to do something that I am not doing myself, which is being vulnerable. Don't lock back up your feelings or put them behind closed doors under lock and key. *You can't heal what you conceal, and you can't restore what you ignore.* Hello, my name is Timothy, and this is a short excerpt of my story.

In boxing, the conditioning that gets you ready for the fight and even the intense training is called roadwork. These are the grueling miles of running, countless squats, crunches, and other workout regimens. It is so easy to fall in love with the technique, the power shots, and finesseful slips. But your lack of road work will tell on a fighter extremely fast. People watching may not see all the times you did the roadwork, but they can surely see in those three-minute rounds when you didn't stick to it. It is frankly not fun at all, but there is no way around it. If you want to be a winner and excel in the sport, you have to invest time. You can step in the gym decked out from head to toe with the most expensive gear, but the equipment doesn't make the fighter, the work does. You can't pay your way out of the gull to continue the fight when you are physically bankrupt and exhausted. Roadwork is a true discipline that demands the boxer to dig deep even at the times they don't want too. Who wants to wake up early in the morning to get the run in before a busy day? Who wants to stick to your macros when you keep getting invited out to eat, only to be tempted to cave in and eat poorly? My strong assumption is that not many people you know would do these things and more, but of course, there are exceptions.

**Rated R**

The emotional and mental roadwork in your life required to find and fight for your healing could be just as grueling. It can be a painful process because you have to face yourself. It refutes running and beckons courage even during times of fear. Maybe your emotional maturity is a lazy couch potato, and the first step to a transformation is putting on your sneakers. Perhaps like many other failed diets and healthy attempts to work out, you use those times to prove that you can't do it because you tried before. How are you going to see the lifestyle change and get to a place of health? There are many steps to take, but the initial leap is possibly the scariest, which is honesty. Your transparency demands you are honest with yourself. The movie of your life is rated R, and the "R" stands for real. You will have to do the emotional, mental, and possibly physical and spiritual road work to get you in shape to stop being your own punching bag.

I am not asking you to do something that I am not willing to do myself, and that is, to open up. This is a hard feat of strength because, like you, it can seem without fail that opening up brings a risk of being bombarded with pain and betrayal. But we can't keep raising the draw bridge of our emotional castle to protect what's inside, all the while what's inside is starving to death; because what it needs is help that it can't get to. With all that said, grab your sneakers and take a run with me as I tell you a part of my story. I warn you; this is rated R. It raw, real, relevant, revealing, and I hope as you read it, it will be refreshing. You are not alone, and you aren't the only ones that have been fighting a fight that is tempting to quit combating. Let's get this roadwork, run with me.

# CHAPTER 8

## PUNCH IN THE GUT

I hate it when I hear someone say that God will not put more on you than you can bear. As the weight of your circumstances is crushing you, this assumingly innocent statement can truly feel unauthentic and void of truth. These last few years felt like I was living the game of "Frogger". Frogger is a video game with a simple task to get on the other side of the road. But the catch is that there is oncoming traffic that isn't stopping for you just because you have a destination in mind. Over and over, you find yourself getting run over. Once you finally make it across the other side, there is only a brief moment to celebrate because you find yourself right back where you started. But this time around, the game got more intense as there is more traffic, and they are moving faster. You must then rely on the lessons and experience you gained in the previous levels to help you beat this one. These last few years have been crushing after crushing, beating after beating, and the desire to quit it all has been intoxicating. I have been pastoring and preaching for over a decade, but let me tell you, that doesn't mean anything when it comes to the mysteries of life. The calling doesn't create a forcefield around me and people like me that makes us void of storms and hardships; frankly, it can feel that it puts me in a spotlight. Every car in this *Frogger* game of life has had a name on it with a goal to crush. My world felt that it was caving in, and it started when my wife was staring at the fear of death face to face.

## Till Death Do Us Part

I wrote my first book called "Crowns Are Greater Than Trophies" and traveled around the nation on a book tour and preaching. I was speaking near Chicago when I received a phone call that she was rushed to the Emergency Room. All kinds of issues were happening to her body all at once. We had no idea what was going on and weren't getting any solid answers. Much of the encounters were attacking the symptoms, but we needed to get to the root of the issue— medication after medication and procedure after procedure and still no closer to any answers. While all of this was happening, she was getting sicker every single day, losing more of her health. Panic was in her voice, and worry was on our minds as we were trying to navigate these untraversed times. It came to the point that she believed that she might be knocking on death's door, but I am thankful to say that she is alive today.

We worked so hard and were on a mission to buy our first house, saved up money, and were ready to step into the new year with expectation. But her sickness threw our entire family in the woodshed where it felt as if life itself had "beef" with us, and it wasn't pulling punches. We ended up finding out that my wife was poisoned by mold. It was everywhere in her body, her blood, the brain, just everywhere. It was affecting different functions in her body and was slowly killing her. While I was at her doctor's appointment, I received a phone call from our landlord that he was selling the house and we had to move out. It felt like the problems were compounding and were frankly overwhelming. We saved up the money to buy a house, but we had to spend it on all the medical expenses trying to find answers. To compound to the issues due to the mold in her body, she has to detox, which demanded a place void of mold and mildew and as close to sterile as possible. We found ourselves between a rock and a hard place. We couldn't just move anywhere, and the cheapest places that we could afford were old and polar opposite of what she needed to detox. We ended up being homeless living in hotels because we couldn't find a home in time. I felt like I was the star on the *Pursuit of Happiness*, trying to make fun memories with my son in the hardest of times. To add fuel to the fire, when I told people about what was happening to my family, some didn't believe us because they never heard of mold in the bloodstream. I am so thankful for the ones that had our back and the community that has been created during these times. However, I never in my life witnessed how some "Christians" dismissed us the way that they did. I entertained the thought of leaving the ministry every single day. I gave my life to the call and helped so many families and foolishly believed that if I was ever in that place, then people would rise and aid us the way we had done for them. I was mistaken, and it was one of the first times that I can remember asking myself the question, am I fighting depression?

A conversation is still seared in my mind, and every time I think about it, the audio is played. I made a post on my social media accounts of my family being homeless, and we were looking for a place to live. I was asked to sit down and talk and was told to delete the word "homeless" because of the reflection it may and is giving. It wasn't how are you doing, how can I help, but your struggle is affecting me. It felt like how some in Christian communities gave my family and me the finger and walked away, yet at the same time, during their trauma, they would walk back to us to help them through their pain. I realized that everyone isn't like me or would treat me the way I have treated them. Let me tell you; I was struggling in these moments with these thoughts and experiences. I didn't understand compartmentalized compassion.

## Strokes

Here I am, standing in a moment of uncertainty, just trying my best to keep it all together. My wife was bedridden and could barely get out of the house, and my son was a little over two years old. I needed to be mom and dad, but I would be lying to you if I would say that it all didn't take a toll on me. I wasn't sleeping, barely eating, and gained a massive amount of weight in a short period of time. I tried to go on a diet to drop the weight, and nothing would really happen. I was doing to exact same things that helped me get in shape in the past. But what made this time in my life different than the past was the massive amount of stress placed on my shoulders.

My wife was starting to get better; just to see her do the everyday task was a testimony and sight to see. As I walked through one storm, here comes another holding on to its coat tail. I get a call that my Dad had three strokes and was in the hospital. I drive to North Carolina to see him, and he had no idea who I was. The strokes cost him his memory and left him with some paralysis. When He saw me, he looked through me and past me, unaware who I was. I already felt like I was barely holding on and keeping myself together, then life tosses another boulder on my shoulders. I want to help my Dad, but how do I do it? Where do I get the money, especially when my wife and kid are still trying to make it through our crises? I drive back to Florida to pick up my family and head back to North Carolina. This time my son is with me along with my wife, and I take them to see my father. Sadly, at that time, there wasn't as much progress. My Dad loves his grandkids and would smile at the thought of them, yet once again has no idea who they are. On that specific drive home, I told my wife that I was going to start boxing. I needed therapy that was going to help me in different areas of my life. I was fighting thoughts that I never imagined I would have as life was crushing me. I needed to fight back, and I can say in many ways that boxing helped change my life. Depression, deep sadness, worry, anxiety, and all their ugly toxic cousins were trying to knock me out, and I needed to fight back.

I am happy to say at the writing of this book; my Dad is doing better. His memory has drastically improved as well as his mobility, but he has some ways to go. I am fighting hard to build our businesses and life to get the funds to help my father get the aid he deserves and needs. Like *Frogger*, I thought I was passing another level only to find another battle the moment I land.

## Miscarriage

A conversation that my wife would have with me during the times that she was sick was her fear that she would be unable to have more kids due to the sickness. Our son would beg us for a brother or sister as he loved the thought of "family" and siblings. After my wife's detox and her health turning around, we got pregnant and were so happy. We told our son, and he was filled with joy and like many families, begin to plan and tell loved ones and friends. Crisis and trauma don't care if you caught your breath from the last fight; it is a full-court press that pressures you at all moments.

I was at another boxing gym with coaches about to spar

a professional heavyweight boxer for the first time. I was so excited, sparred a few 3 min rounds, and sat down to recover and let other people spar. My phone rang from my gym bag, and I received the dreaded phone call, " I think we lost the baby". I packed my stuff up and ran home, praying and hoping that she was mistaken. What am I going to do? How to I console her? What do I tell our son? Hezekiah was already talking to her belly, falling in love with his future brother or sister. I asked God over and over why He is doing or allowing all of these things to happen to my family. I had to leave out of town to preach at a church in Indiana. I preached in the morning, and in the evening, I was going to preach at a Spanish church. After worship and a few minutes before I was supposed to grab the microphone to speak, my wife calls me. It is confirmed we did lose the baby and had a miscarriage. My world was spinning out of control, and my thoughts felt like they were covered with baby oil, I attempted to reach for them and get it under control, but it was slipping through my fingers. At this moment, I did something that is scary now that I look back at it. Remember, I am seconds away from preaching life and hope to the people in the congregation. I detached myself from my pain and situation, completely compartmentalized it, and preached the gospel bypassing my own emotions. I have gotten so use to not feeling my feeling that I could turn a switch on and go through the motions of preaching while emotionally, I was a wreck.

There is a term called "Smiling Depression," which simply coins the actions of someone who has a smile on their face and outwardly appears happy yet is fighting depression. Not only do they have a smile on their faces, but they can strive to put a smile on others. People around them may never know they are fighting because they cover it up so well. These people can typically be the "strong" people in your life. They are often the first ones to reach out to someone if they need help, the first to send a text, and much more. The fuel to these actions can be that they know what depression and hurt feel like, and they don't want someone else to experience it. You need to make sure you are checking up on your "strong" friends and family because they may be fighting a deep, painful, and lonely battle. Smiling depression is very real, and I am confident that preaching depression is real as well. The Christian community is filled with it, and don't even know it at times. My faith in Christ should not be my excuse for me to not feel my feelings but to work and process them. Nor are the moments that you refuse to feel your feelings the signs that you are more like Christ. There are so many toxic behaviors and actions that have been adopted in the Christian community, many of which I am striving to unlearn.

I could go on and on with stories from these past two years and fill this entire book. I am sure you have your own highlight reels of crisis that have occurred in your life. You may be asking why did I include this chapter in this book? There are many reasons, but to name a few, I want to model to you that it is ok to be transparent. It is ok to tell your story and get used to talking about the things that are happening. Your real-life isn't Instagram, where you just post the great things that are happening. Your life is hard, you have been through some mess, and you are trying your best to hold it all together. It is liberating to talk about your battles to the right people in the correct spaces. You have kept your lips sealed and your healing at bay. I know it is taboo nowadays for people to be transparent about their feelings and experiences, but you can't let that stop you. I have attended many funerals of someone who died from suicide during the years and can't tell you the number of times I have heard people say, " I didn't know it was that bad". For some, that may be true because the victim hid their battle so well. For others, it could be that they didn't pause long enough to see the red flags of the people hurting around them. We live in such a fast-paced society that we can forget to stop and see the individuals around us.

**Punch In The Gut**

Oftentimes in boxing, when sparring and fighting, the fighter can become what some have called a "headhunter". This is when you are throwing all of your punches and shots at the person's head, but you neglect their body. Yes, a knockout can occur when a good shot is landed, but there are many fights that are won when the boxer knocks the wind out of the other fighter. The punch in the gut, liver shots, and other hits to the body can lay the fighter out on the canvas in the fetal position, hugging their sides rocking back and forth. Sometimes it is not a single strong punch that does the job but the consistent hit to the same place on the body to break down until they are broken down.

Protect yourself at all times because life can hit you where it hurts, and don't let up. It is tempting to stay down because you feel like at least you won't get hit again. But that is the place it wants you at, to quit and give up. To get comfortable detaching yourself from the goal to win and the effort required to conquer. Get back up; the countdown is still happening. I know it is hard, and you are tired, but you can win this as you yourself become the consistent weapon aiming tactically at the areas of your emotional, mental, chemical, or spiritual conflict. Punch depression in the gut and knock the wind out of it to continue. Get the help you need and remove the air it needs to survive. Give yourself a breath of fresh air by being intentional to talk about your feelings and the issues you are facing. I became a Life Coach because I want to be the person in your corner, passionately shouting encouragement and guidance while helping you meet the right people to help you win. Stand up, catch your breath, put your gloves up, and get back in the fight. Use your jab so you can make sure that what you are fighting on the outside of you doesn't get in the inside of you.

# CHAPTER 9

## TRAINING PARTNER

Have you ever been around a group of people, yet you still feel that you are alone? Do you know what it is to fight internally just to force yourself to smile while deep inside you want to shut down? Every day you look in the mirror and coach yourself just to make it through another day. At the end of the day, you are exhausted, not because of the workload but also because of enduring the effort required to force a smile to benefit the people around you. You have become a master at shifting conversations when people pry into your well-being because you are scared of the rush of feelings and tears that may erupt. You have to build a dam of boundaries and borders around your emotions because you know if it is broken, you don't know how to handle or process the flood. You have become so good at masking your feelings just to survive that you have a hard time knowing when to open up or how to? Does any of these describe you? Have you felt any of these ways in your life? Many people have, and every single day, they wake up and dress up the avatar representing them so their true self can remain protected, yet it will stay broken. Sometimes these are learned behaviors and actions because it is easier to accept that "it is what it is" or, in other words, " this is how it is always going to be." The temptation to just accept existing instead of living is how we tell ourselves that it is ok, because we have tried before. **Failed efforts are an intoxicating drug that keeps procrastination addicted to excuses.** It's 100% proof bootleg moonshine that burns going down, that serenades a lullaby of acceptance, that ends the day hungover and regret.

Maybe you are reading this book, and you are the person that has already told yourself that it is pointless for you to get help because you deemed yourself hopeless. Are you the reader that has already told yourself that seeking therapy isn't a good idea because "they are just going to tell you things you already know"? This kind of thinking is a hindrance to your freedom from this slave driver called depression. **When we lose the will to try, we forfeit the chance to win.** I want to be very clear in what I am saying and stating. I am by no means telling you that what you are feeling and how you are feeling isn't justified. I am not saying that you don't deserve to feel the way you do. I am saying and attempting to relay to you the importance to keep trying even when you want to quit. It is tough to muster up the strength to apply effort to a thing that seems pointless. What makes it even more difficult is when you feel that the people around you have abandoned you. Maybe when you first told people how you were doing, they reached out to you with concern. And now those same people aren't answering your texts or calls. You have pondered, "maybe I am a burden to them" or " they don't care anymore". Adding fuel to the fire, these kinds of thoughts thus drive you further into anxiety and depression. There is a man in the Christian Bible that has an experience that I believe many can understand. He found himself in need but felt abandoned and forgotten.

## I Have No One

John 5:1-9 NKJV

*5 After this there was a feast of the Jews, and Jesus went up to Jerusalem. 2 Now there is in Jerusalem by the Sheep Gate a pool, which is called in Hebrew, Bethesda, having five porches. 3 In these lay a great multitude of sick people, blind, lame, paralyzed, waiting for the moving of the water. 4 For an angel went down at a certain time into the pool and stirred up the water; then whoever stepped in first, after the stirring of the water, was made well of whatever disease he had. 5 Now a certain man was there who had an infirmity thirty-eight years. 6 When Jesus saw him lying there, and knew that he already had been in that condition a long time, He said to him, "Do you want to be made well?"*

*7 The sick man answered Him, "Sir, I have no man to put*

*me into the pool when the water is stirred up; but while I am coming, another steps down before me."*

*8 Jesus said to him, "Rise, take up your bed and walk." 9 And immediately the man was made well, took up his bed, and walked.*

Can you imagine the mental, emotional, spiritual, and physical strain that had to take place in his life? Every time the angel stirred the water, and he had a moment to get his healing, someone else got ahead of him. The toll that must have taken on him and the temptation to just accept the outcome of his life must have been alluring. At first glance of the story, we can foolishly read it and count out the man for making excuses. Standing here void from the experience of being in his shoes we can say, "I would have done such and such," or "If he would have just done...." We can attempt to point fingers at the man, assuming he lacked effort. I don't read about a man making excuses, I see a man speaking his truth, something that all of us need to learn how to do better.

When the man at the pool said he had no one, he didn't mean that there was no one around him; he was saying that there was no one willing to get involved. There's plenty of people laid out around him. There's plenty of non-disabled people helping other people get into the pool; he wasn't saying that no one around had the strength; he believed the people around him didn't have or make the availability. What he was lacking was community and people in his life that were willing to stick with him in his journey of healing.

" I have no one" wasn't an excuse; it was his truth.

## Community

He was in desperate need of community, people, or even a person that was aware of what he needed and willing to stick with him during the journey. If you are someone who doesn't struggle with mental health in these areas and are reading this book to help someone, then let me first tell you thank you. Secondly, please know that if you are going to tell that person that you will walk with them, then do so and be consistent. The last thing that they need is another person giving empty promises and misleading hope. The fact that you decided to pick up this book or listen to the audiobook deserves a pat on the back. I am so proud of you that you are mustering up the strength to contend for your healing even after all of this time. It is so easy to give up and accept an outcome that hasn't happened yet. The man lying by the pool had the issues for over thirty-eight years; however, he still gave effort when the angel stirred the water. I don't know your story or the details of your battle, but one thing that I do know is that it wasn't easy to make up in your mind and heart to keep fighting forward.

I encourage you to be vocal, active, and intentional to build a community of people around you that are aware of your fight with anxiety, depression, deep sadness, and other emotions. I strongly encourage you to seek professional help if you need it, and don't overlook the power and peace that friendship can usher into your life.

Whether you are going to be the friend or in need of that friend, be attentive, and get involved. **Depression will use abandonment as a petri dish growing in every silent and inactive area it touches.** There is power in having a community, a flashlight held in darkness, throwing its light in your direction.

**5 Recommendations for The Friend**

If you are a friend or loved one reading this book with the hope to help the one in need, here are five recommendations to help you help them.

1) Take Initiative

Take the initiative to reach out even before they ask for your help or even if it seems like they don't need it. It is easy to " fake it till you make it" when it comes to mental health until you just can't fake it anymore. Some people have been so accustomed to painting makeup on their well-being every morning that they have difficulty removing it to get to their truth. When you walk through life, assuming that no one cares and believe that you have proof that no one cares, it's easy to live in that realm of thinking. But you will be the one that proves them wrong; some people care, and one of those people is you. Taking the initiative to reach out and offering your help is beyond a single text, phone call, or conversation, but many. You may have to be a drill bit constantly reaching out to dig deep through the hardened layers of protection they have created through the years. Remember, sometimes to hope again is to risk pain again, and the walls and "fronts" created are tiers of their security.

## 2) Be Consistent

If they have graced you with the privilege to step past the boundaries and borders erected around their life, it is a gift. This gift and opportunity will be squandered if you aren't attentive and consistent. I am not saying that you have enlisted yourself to become their indentured servant, but the words " I am here for you" shouldn't be empty but full of conviction and follow through. Maybe it is a text once a week or a facetime schedule that y'all set up. Maybe it is a phone call marked on your calendars or planned outings. It is vital that you make time instead of finding time so that consistency will be kept. They are used to people walking in and out of their life; please don't be the next one on the list. This is different for every person, but you will help both of you win when you ask and plan rather than assume and perceive.

## 3) Expectations

Ask the simple question, " What do you need from me?" Lay it all out on the table and help build the outcome together. Be prepared for the response to be "I don't know," as they may not really know. Even in that, there is a beauty at the moment to discover it together. I don't believe it is wise to walk into the journey with your own preconceived ideas and goals and place it on their shoulders to bear. Maybe they just want your presence to be around, and maybe they want a person to text and call when they feel a panic attack coming. When you ask for expectations, this also gives you a chance to say yes or no to the things you can and can't do. There is peace and security when they know that they have access to an ear that will listen when they share their heart and feelings.

4) Do Research

Read books, watch shows, and study what they are fighting to help equip and aid them. I like to send Tic Talks, Instagram, and YouTube videos that show practical exercises like breathing and taps that help control or mitigate anxiety and panic attacks. I like to do these things before they ask and throughout the week for many reasons. I want them to know that I care and show the fruit of it. I want them to know that I am on their side to fight back and through the fight of depression and anxiety. There are plenty of great books to share with them, including this one (see what I did there) that can help them. When you commit to being with them, don't just let it be about words but actions. You may not be the psychologist, therapist, life coach, or pastor, but you can be the friend, which is powerful.

5) Be A Safe Place

A title that I hold dearly is when leaders and people call me Alcatraz because of my legal and ethical confidentiality standards. They call me Alcatraz because the information comes in but doesn't come out. I hold this dear and as a badge of honor because I believe in being trustworthy and a man of my word. When I sit down with someone and share my heart, I expect that I will not see it on social media and gossip about it.

I hope this is unnecessary to say, but please don't be a gossiper and an untrustworthy person. If they are confiding in you, Facebook doesn't need to know what they are saying. The caveat in all of this is to know when you need to get extra help. When someone is talking about harming themselves or others, then you may need to seek professional help.

## 5 Recommendations for You

The man lying at the pool for all of those years felt forgotten, overlooked, and ignored. When Jesus came to help and asked him questions, he could have stayed silent and assumed that it would be a pointless conversation. But because he spoke up, that encounter changed his life. It is hard to do, but we must not let pain and fear derived from past experiences place tape on our lips and keep the chance of transformation shut up and shut out. Sometimes when you are feeling all alone, it may indicate that you are alone. If you have people reaching out to you to help or strive to reach out, here are five recommendations to keep in mind.

### 1) Speak up

You are going to have to speak up about what you need and what you are going through. This can be scary for many reasons, but if you are going to allow the vetted person in your life, they need to know how to aid you. One of the many dangers of smiling depression is that it risks the chance that you won't be asked if you need help because people assume you don't need it. If possible, muster up the courage to speak openly and honestly to your friends about what is happening. You may be amazed that they are fighting the same fights or maybe fought their way out of it. There is an old saying which goes, "a closed mouth won't get fed." Perhaps this isn't a social media post but a direct message. Maybe it's not shouting from the rooftops but a one-on-one conversation. You may be thinking that no one cares when you have been faking for so long and so well that no one is aware; when you are asked " how are you doing," give it a try and honestly tell that person striving to build community with you how you are doing.

2) Don't Hide or Runaway

I want to encourage you to not go back into hiding or runway when things get serious. Avoidance can be a coping mechanism that is tempting to let lead and rule your life. It is a Siren continuing her serenades, enticing you into the deep waters of fear only to be devoured by hopelessness. It wants to keep you far from your help, not close to it. But how can you fix, heal, and recover from any issues that you spend time acting as if it doesn't exist? It is tempting to run away or to avoid community altogether because it may feel that confronting the roots and trauma may be more exhausting than running away from it. Run towards help, not away from it, run towards prayer, not away from it. Run towards a well-intended healthy community, not away from it. One of my favorite verses is Psalms 121:1-2, which says, "*I lift up my eyes to the mountains where does my help come from? 2 My help comes from the Lord, the Maker of heaven and earth.*"

## 3) Follow Through

I know I am risking sounding like a broken record, but I don't want to risk me sounding as if I am insensitive to your feelings and experiences. I know that depression can make the simplest of task, such as taking a shower or getting out of bed, daunting and difficult. Do what you can when you can but strive to follow through with what you have committed yourself to do. Maybe you learned that breathing exercises help with anxiety, and friends searched for that information for you. Give it a try; just maybe it will help you. Be willing to take risks towards your journey of healing and betterment. You spoke up and asked for help, and someone responded and was a right fit to help. They can be the right person for the right task, but if you slap their hands away, they can't do anything. Do what you can, in the limit you can, when you can, and watch growth and progress start to occur.

## 4) Lean on Them

Have you been so accustomed to doing everything yourself that you don't know how to utilize the help around you? Lean on the community around you and let them help you. Whether that is your therapist, Life Coach, psychologist, pastor, loved ones, choose to give them a chance to help you.

Here is the mental tug of war that can occur that may not be rooted in truth but in fear. What if you ask too much and they leave? What if you lean on them too much and the weight of your problems crush them? What if you come across as needy you may ask? Remember they reached out to you to see how they can help? You aren't needy; you are someone that is in need, and they want to be of service. You aren't talking to strangers; you are talking with people that value you and want you to win and succeed.

## 5) Be Consistent

It is extremely hard to drive a nail with a hammer with only one swing. But a consistent tap of the hammer can drive a nail in wood. When I think of achieving breakthrough, this is the imagery that comes to my mind. Maybe what you needed to help you overcome this giant of anxiety and depression wasn't simply to get stronger, but what if it was to become consistent. When you have a community of people that are aware of your struggle and fight, they can help you stay consistent in your efforts. Maybe on one day, it is easier than other days to get up and drive yourself to a counseling session, but now you have a friend to call that could take you and encourage you on the way. The old adage how do you eat an elephant, one bite at a time rings true with so many things in life. Allow your community to be a safety net to catch you when you fall and aid you in standing back up to fight another day.

## Can I Get A Spot

Working out can be hard and challenging in and of itself. It takes discipline and consistency to get in shape and stay in shape. I used to have a workout partner named Dennis that absolutely pushed me to my limits in the weight room. He is a gifted bodybuilder and won shows from the first time he stepped on the stage. I learned a lot from him during our workouts in the gym, and I learned many life lessons in the iron jungle. Before I started to work out with him, I thought that working out was just lifting up heavy things and putting them down, but it is more than that. He told me that I need to feel the muscle and engage it, a term called Mind and Muscle Connection. To work out and get the most out of it required a level of mental focus. They engaged the correct muscle and focused on the intensity. Without mind and muscle connection, you can just throw the weight up and not feel the pump in the specific area that you are targeting. You can see this a lot on the bench press when people unrack the barbell, lower it down quickly and bounce the bar off their chest. Yes, they got the weight up, but did they target the chest correctly. Don't get me wrong, sometimes life is like a powerlifter, and you have to throw the weight off you. But if you are trying to sculpt the target area, it takes mental attention and physical strain. So, where is the life lesson with mind and muscle connection? When you are working out and under heavyweight, a keen focus is required. I know so much of what you have been fighting in life can feel like it was trying to crush you.

Nothing is more of a grueling exercise than a movement called a "Negative." This movement and motion will take all the strength you have. We did it at the end of the workout to use up whatever we had left in the tank. You can do negatives with many different lifts, but one of the most grueling was when we did it on the bench press to end a workout. There will be a person behind the bench called a spotter. They then will help you unrack the weight with typically a heavier amount that you can generally press up, and hand it to you at the top of your lift. Unlike the regular bench press that you lower down then lift back up, you move as slow as you can or for a specific count until it touches your chest. When it reaches your chest, you don't try to push it up; your spotter lifts it off of you and helps you bring it back to the starting position to do it again. The entire workout is about time under tension. So, where is the life lesson in all of this? It is amazing how learning how to lift negative weight can have positive results. It's time under the tension that tears the muscles down, setting the stage for it to grow back even stronger. It is an act of strength when we in life can learn how to use our negative experiences like a gym, work out through them to get positive strength. A strength that can create compassion, a strength that can give clarity to one's purpose. Typically, all of these works require a spotter, someone there to help lift the weight in your times of failure or when you have no strength left.

A training partner can help you stay on task and fight through the times when you don't have any desire to get up and workout. I believe it is so important to find community and create a community around you that knows your goals. Depression, anxiety, deep sadness, among other emotions and feelings, can fester in isolation. When you take the risk to let trusted and vetted people in and aware of your fight, they can help you lift the weight and become stronger during the process. Boxing is a demanding sport and demands attention and dedication. It is great when you have someone in your corner, helping you stay on track. Sure, you can train alone, but the great thing about life and community, especially when you find the right people is that you don't have to.

**It's Scary**

I know it is scary to try again, to love again, to hope again. It is scary to make up in your mind to let people in your life because you are concerned about the mess they may make along the way. I would just ask you to not only think about what could go wrong but what can go right. Your life can change when you choose to take your pain out of the privacy of darkness and bring it into the light. My hope for you is that people love you are chasing after you and that you will slow down enough for them to catch up. It may be scary right now, but I am hoping that your horror movie turns into an action movie where you fight back to a love story where you find peace, happiness, and joy.

# CHAPTER 10

# ENOUGH

There is no pretty way to put it, but there are times in your life that you have to draw the line and say enough is enough. Many things in life can be harmful to your mental, emotional, physical, and spiritual health. In 2002 a movie came out starring Jennifer Lopez called *Enough*. She was a woman who fell in love with a man, but he would become a deadbeat man, physically and emotionally abusing her. When it first started to happen, she was in shock and didn't know what to do or where to go. But she soon arrived at the place in her life that she knew that enough is enough. She knew that wishful thinking wasn't going to free her from the jaws of that monster, but she needed to know how to fight back. She enlisted herself in training and intense workouts with a mission and a goal.

She made up in her mind that she wasn't going to be a doormat or a punching bag. She knew that it was time for her to punch back, use her jab, and contend with escaping his clutch. Words weren't going to make a difference at this moment, and tears weren't going to move him emotionally to self-examine his actions.

The figurative bell rang like in boxing matches, and the fight was on. She made the first move, drawing the line and letting her intentions known. He tried to laugh it off as if it was a joke but soon found out that she was serious; she had enough. He was physically larger than her and stronger than her, but she didn't let that stop her. Her training was paying off as she was striking and slipping, keeping her hands in a position that she was ready for whatever could come at her. He was attempting to grab her aggressively and swung punches wildly, expecting things to go as they did in the past. But he wasn't dealing with the same person; she had a mission and a goal. She wasn't backing down; she was going to beat him down. Minutes passed in the brawl and he finally got ahold of her, pinning her against the wall, attempting to choke her out. It was this same position that traumatized her in the past, but she knew what to do. She slams her elbow at the pivot of his elbow, freeing herself from his grip. This man was a coward, a physically strong person but an insanely weak man that thrived on control and hitting her and people when they were down. When she was knocked down on the floor after he hit her from behind on the head with a lamp, he thought it was his chance to finish her, but he was wrong. He believed that it was his moment to hit her when she was down and let her know once again who the boss was, stroking his own ego and creating a false sense of manhood derived from cowardice. As she lay on the ground, aware that he was going to kick her when she was down, she strikes first and wins the fight. At the end of this, she would walk away from this abusive marriage with her daughter Grace and the fortitude to know that she will never be a victim again.

Maybe your life doesn't look like the movie *Enough*, but maybe you simply are living in a place where you had enough. She couldn't progress forward in life until she removed herself from the toxic environment that she was in. As you are on a mission to take back your mental, physical, spiritual, and emotional health, you must give attention to your environment as well as your influences. Maybe it isn't physically fighting your way out but having tough conversations. Maybe it isn't learning how to throw a hook and counters but self-care and self-love. It may not be slipping and evading but taking inventory of the people you call friends and family and how they are treating you. The bottom line is that you must create boundaries in your life because you may be in a toxic environment that is feeding depression, anxiety, and all the other issues you are striving to overcome.

**Cut It Off**

In 2003 a man named Aron Lee Ralston's life would change forever as he stared at the possibility of death face to face. Aron was an outdoorsman that enjoyed his time out and about in nature, hiking, and climbing mountains. While climbing a mountain in Utah, a boulder shifted and trapped his right wrist. He struggled to free himself and watched as not only time passed by but also his energy. He knew that if he was going to save his life, he would have to free himself from the environment and rock that he was connected to. He had a dull pocketknife and proceeded to cut off his right wrist, freeing himself and remarkably climbed down the mountain to get help and medical attention.

What are you connected to that is unhealthy and toxic to your well-being and health? What environments are you in or have you created that are seeping out the seams with negativity and trauma-inducing actions? You have a responsibility to yourself to look around and to look within to assess that you may need to make the change. Like many things in life, this is by far easier said than done. You may be reading this and telling yourself that "you don't understand; it's not that simple." You are right that it isn't that simple, as there could be many variables connected to your situation's dynamics. What if the person that is holding the hands of conflict is a member of your family? What if it is a workplace and you told yourself that you couldn't quit because you have to pay the bills? There can be mountain-sized reasons or excuses. We can all make a list, but one thing is for sure, there needs to be a change. I will not insult you with an attempt to water down the risk you may feel or the anxiety connected to the thought. In fact, I will confront a lie that you may have been telling yourself and allowed it to court your fear and date your procrastination. The lie is that you can't create boundaries in your life because it will cause division to the people around you. You have been told during the times that you expressed how you felt that you are wrong to feel that way and to just deal with it. You have been told so often that you accepted it so many times as truth when it is a lie. These kinds of words can be from friends, family, and loved ones. Words that can feel like ropes tying you to a chair like a hostage, forced to watch the willpower beaten out of it. You aren't creating a division with that person that is cussing at you and always yelling when you tell them to stop; you are stating your boundaries. It is often the perpetrator of pain and wrongdoings that will say to the victim that they are causing division and overreacting. I have been pastoring for over a decade and have had many people's families in my office. It has always saddened me when I have parents in my office that don't understand this as it creates further separation between them and their children.

The parent can feel like they have a God-given right to yell at their kids, be mean, cuss and degrade them and believe that it's ok because they are their parents. Then the moment the child speaks up, even at a young age, that they are hurt, the child is then reprimanded and corrected because they are speaking up. The parent then says that they are being disrespectful and causing division in the household when, in fact, they are just trying to speak up for themselves. All this does is continue the cycle of trauma and unchecked issues that they experienced. Parents, we do not own our children; we are called to steward, love, and raise them. All those years, parents unknowingly or aware of the fact would have sown division, and the moment the child comes of age to move out, they see the harvest of it; separation and avoidance. They wonder why they don't call as often or why they aren't telling them about their problems when it's because they feel like it isn't a safe place to do so. Coming of age wasn't just about maturity for those children, but a chance to escape the pollution spewed from the smokestacks of malicious mouths for decades.

There are many areas in life that you have to learn how to put your wellbeing first and create boundaries. Work, church, loved ones, family members, just to name a few, are not inherently wrong but could be a space for toxic environments. Navigate every area of your life as you traverse different settings to ensure your health is intact. When the doctors have to cut out the cancerous tumor, they separate and divide the patient from the issue. The cut is needed and painful, but the host will die without attention to the issue at hand. **Those claiming division may perceive you are swinging a sword when, in fact, you are wielding a scalpel making incisions of boundaries, cutting away the tumor, saving your mental, physical, emotional, and even spiritual health.**

**Appetite**

We must always give attention to the environment we are forced to be around and the spaces we are drawn toward. Sometimes we can spend so much time pointing fingers at everyone else that we don't take the time to look in the mirror. Why are you drawn to the bar and other people drinking their problems away? Why are you drawn to toxic relationships that use you for your body but negates your heart, emotions, and spirit? Why do you feel the need to cut yourself and other acts of self-harm to feel better? Why do you have an appetite for things that offer temporary satisfaction only to yield subpar results? These are hard questions to present to ourselves, but it is a journey that should be taken. These are some of the many reasons why having a Therapist, Psychologist, Life Coach, and or Pastor is important to have that can help you in the journey. People called to these occupations can be like your Tour Guide driving through your wilderness, taking you on a journey of introspection. Once you discover the root of your "why," clarity is often the pot of gold found at the end of the rainbow. Sometimes we can be lured into destruction by our own appetites.

I once heard a story that illustrates the danger of being self-destructive from the enticement of our vices. There once was a village in a cold and frozen part of the world that kept getting attacked by ravaging wolves. The wolves would go into the camp at night and kill their livestock and even hunt their children. The villagers came up with a great idea to create boundaries around the village by using the wolves' own appetites for blood against them. They killed an animal, took the blood, and plastered it all over the blades of double edge swords. They then waited until the blood froze on the swords to add another application of blood. They did this over and over until the sword was thick and layered, making a bloody, sharp popsicle. They planted the swords' handles all around the village with only the bloody blades emerged from the ground. Finally, the sun had set, and the nocturnal hunters went on the prowl to kill and fill their stomachs at the village. But this time, when they came to the village, they smelled the alluring fragrance of blood emanating from the sword blades. The wolves then began to lick the blood from the blades repeatedly until their tongues were numb from the ice and cold. They kept licking, tasting blood until all of a sudden, they tasted warm blood, which pushed them to lick with more fervency. Unbeknown to them, they licked away all the frozen blood layers until the sword cut their own tongues as they drunk their own blood. Once they were full of blood, they left with serrated tongues, walking away from the village to later be found dead from bleeding out. They became their own worse enemies, and all the villagers had to do was capitalize on their appetite and desires.

So the question remains; What is in me that is attracted to unhealthy atmospheres, lifestyles, and actions? Why am I lured into the destructive hands of self-sabotage from personal vices? It could be for many reasons, but here is one that deserves attention. It could be that you are chasing after things that help you not "feel your feelings" or simply escape them. Are you accustomed to reaching for a bottle of liquor to drown your sorrows when in fact, you need to talk about them? Are you used to eating your problems away instead of working through them? Now you may not want to hear this, but it must be said. Have you been using church and God as a way of escape and not as places of restoration? Have you been using the high of a shout and dance of a Sunday morning in the same way the addict in the ally uses heroin to shoot up so they won't have to feel? Have you been shouting about things that you aren't willing to fight for? Have you been running to the gym because you are running away from the problems you don't want to face or feel? I wish I were sitting right in front of you to hear your story and give detailed advice. This is why I love being a Life Coach that helps people traverse the hardships of life. *But what I can tell you is this, sometimes you need to make boundaries around yourself, from yourself.*

### Side Step

In your endeavors to create a safe space for you to heal and deal with your mental health, examine the environment around you and in you. It is a place in your life you may be saying to yourself that you can't wait to move out. Surely, the change or location may help, but what if the issues at hand weren't solely the place but the person? Let's say that you are living in a place infested with roaches and bugs. You load up your U-haul with all your baggage and stuff and move into a new home thousands of miles away. Once you arrive, you unload all your baggage into your new home only to find out days later that this place has roaches too. You get angry at first, thinking to yourself that you have bad luck by moving into a home that also has a roach problem. You call the landlord, and they tell you that they never had a problem before, and they are just as perplexed as you. You now feel like Sherlock Holmes starting your own investigation as you walk through the house. Suddenly, you discover the answer to the plight you were facing has been facing you all along. There were roaches and eggs living in the furniture and baggage that you carried with you from one end of the country to the other. If only you had dealt with your baggage, you wouldn't have carried over the problem. This is what it looks like when we try to blame our way to the journey of healing. Yes, there are responsibilities in other people's hands, but just running away and changing locations won't always create the space and place you need to heal. At the risk of sounding hypocritical and counter everything I just said, on the other hand, you best believe that moving and changing environments can be the fresh start and change you need to kick start your healing.

Boxing is a demanding sport because it continually requires being active in both offense and defense. A foundational move I was taught pertaining to footwork was the sidestep. The sidestep is both an evasive move and step-creating angles to land punches and counter. The sidestep can create both angles and create distance. It can create an angle to slip through defense and evade punches coming from the opponent. A good sidestep and a solid jab can make you a force to be reckoned with because you can create distance and boundaries while staying in the fight. The goal in boxing is to land punches without getting punched, and solid footwork helps with that. A sidestep isn't running away, but it is repositioning. Creating boundaries in your life isn't running away or retreating; it rushes towards your health and moves for healing. Grab the jump rope and work on your footwork because it is time to practice evasive drills. You are going to fight forward and position yourself to win.

# CHAPTER 11

# COMBOS

W hen I decided to write this book, I had a primary goal. A goal that can seem simple when written out on paper but can be extremely difficult to apply. An action that can be overlooked and deemed unimportant even though it is necessary for growth and healing. It has been a repeated request throughout the pages of this book. The task that I am referring to is talking. Yes, speaking up and speaking out about the issues you are fighting in private is vital to your growth and healing process. For many reasons, maybe you have counseled yourself to believe that keeping quiet is the best option for you. Maybe because of all the times you have felt betrayed by other people. Perhaps, you don't believe you have a safe person to approach or the notion that no one cares in the first place. There could be a mountain size list of reasons that we tell ourselves to zip our lips, but we must climb to the top to gain a healthy perspective. When writing this book, I hoped that you wouldn't simply feel that you have arrived at your final destination or breakthrough after reading this book but be courageous to start your journey. Yes, of course, I am hoping for healing along the way as you turn every page, but maybe you need to take steps to stop internalizing your pain but vocalizing it. I launched my Life Coaching business because of this very same thing. I witness how people were crushed from internalization, living beneath their purpose feeling lost. I witnessed perceived successful people playing emotional Marco Polo with their peace of mind. I chatted with people that could buy their world but lost the things that meant the world to them in the process. I recalled the countless hours spent in my office hearing people and families' stories of trauma and pain but lied to themselves faking a smile to keep up with the Joneses. Traveling around the world, speaking and preaching, I get the chance to be an ear to many in leadership and authority. Frequently, on the car ride from the airport to my hotel, tears are already rolling down their faces as they express to me that they feel crushed with stress and church hurt with the belief that they have nowhere to go. There is so much trauma that has happened and is happening in people's lives around the world. Maybe you are saying, "but Timothy, all of this is easier said than done." To that, I would say that is correct. It is by far easier said than done, but it must be done and done now.

**An Oasis of Hope**

I travel around the nation and frequently make history by being the first person of color to preach behind the pulp in a predominantly white church. Being the only person of color in a community and having hard conversations about race, color, and reconciliation, among other things. I remember being on a search to find a therapist and voice to bring into my life to help me work through the trauma and issues of racist attacks and the challenges of being a black man in America. I am a 6' 6" tall 330 lbs. black man raised in the south. I have had more racist encounters than I can list and my fair share of extreme disappointment with the church and their responses. My mom is old enough to remember being told that she couldn't drink from white people's water fountains or shop in there stores. Chased by the KKK, my grandfather would hide in the woods traveling past decaying, lynched black bodies hanging from trees. The south can feel like a time machine that stays unmoved as the world attempts to progress. I still remember this song taught by a white teacher in elementary school, "Cotton needs pickin so bad, cotton need pickin so bad, cotton need pickin so bad we gone pick all over dem fields." I grew up having encounters with racism, but I was shot down every time I would open my mouth, saying it isn't real anymore. So, I told myself that no one cares, and I will have to deal with it alone. I said to myself that I would just "fake it till I make it" while hoping for a day that I can share my pain to progress towards healing. I believed a lie at an early age that I shouldn't talk about my pain and just suck it up and deal with it. My guess is that you have told yourself the same lie over and over also. You don't have to just deal with it; you can face it, confront it, and overcome it, but you need to speak up about it.

In 2020 Black Lives Matter protest launched to another level and gained worldwide momentum. Black Lives Matter is a movement that is directed to end police brutality among other issues of injustices and inequality. When it first started to gain attention and people started to talk about it, I was excited because I thought that the white churches and multi-ethnic churches lead by white leadership would be a safe place for me and people like me to find healing. I was wrong, so wrong, and it was an extreme disappointment that further highlighted the theory that some people don't care about our pain. Or that someone people had no idea what to do with it or where to start. Mind you, I am a preacher and a minister and travel the world and served as a local staff pastor. Churches all around the world became an unsafe place for many black people, minorities, and people of color to heal. I am aware that what I am saying is not true for every church and all leadership. I am aware that every BIPOC (black, indigenous, People of Color) may not carry these thoughts and truths or beliefs. I am thankful that some churches and leaders have been active in ushering healing into so many people's pain. However, before all the attention to the pain in our communities was becoming mainstream conversation, we would be able to give people the benefit of the doubt that they were unaware of what was happening. But once they became aware, many other people and I saw that they just don't care or don't know how to care. I watched as people were leaving churches in masses, trying to find a safe place that Jesus' gospel message was preached and applied to everyone. A place that they felt that the verse "come all who are heavy laden, and I will give you rest" (Matthew 11:28) wouldn't have perceived addendums stating, "but you." **Countless sermons were preached against Black Lives Matter without any attention to heal the pain that mattered to black lives.** Fox News's Laura Ingraham told NBA star Lebron James to shut up and dribble when he spoke about injustices. Many people were told the same thing, from other people to shut up and preach, shut up and teach, shut up and play the keyboard, shut up and drum, shut up and dance, shut up and (you fill in the blank). Many people in the white communities were facing issues also as they processed new information for the first time or saw injustices through a different light. Some began a healing journey for themselves and spoke up only to be attacked and encounter traumatic experiences.

Nationalistic Christianity swept through the nation like a plague causing the hunt for a healthy church for many people in the Christian community even harder. It was an extremely disheartening moment in history that created even more PTSD in our communities. Even though conversations were taking place about mental health, it left people in a dilemma where they knew that they needed help but didn't have a place to go. Where do you go where you don't have to first fight through the mire of proving your pain is legitimate and deserves attention, to the person that is placed there to counsel, pastor, or parent? Or greeted with other churches defense mechanisms of malicious silence, and escapism masquerading as faith to avoid addressing current events? The church of America was bleached of its color in 2020 due to actions or inactivity. People, both white, black, and all other colors and ethnicities choose to create boundaries for their health, even at the risk of calling it, division. People were tired of being greeted with "but what about" when they expressed their pain, fear, and trauma when they simply needed someone to be present and aware. I can write an entire book on these issues alone, and in fact, I may do that.

This is why I launched "TMM Oasis"; An Oasis of hope in a desert of hopelessness," a space that you can find vetted therapists, psychologists, counselors, and other voices and professionals that you can trust will have your best interest in mind. Voices and practices which can help you walk through racism, hate crimes, family conflict, and the laundry list of issues feeding into your depression, anxiety, and health. I launched this space because there was a time that I felt hopeless and abandoned by the church and the fellowship, left alone with my pain without a hospital bed to heal. At TMM Oasis, there is a growing list of professionals from different walks of life. Black, Brown, People of Color, minorities as well as the white communities will have space and a place that they know will provide professionals aware of the different kinds of trauma that you face that you don't have to prove your worthy of healing before you can heal.

I am aware that different kinds of people from different walks of life may grab this book. Maybe these last few pages you were rolling your eyes thinking that this is foolish. But at the same time, there is a reader right now with tears rolling down their faces baptizing the pages of this book, saying "finally" under their breath. This will be a safe place and a healthy space for you to speak up without the fear of being told to shut up.

## Snowflake

I heard a term being used repeatedly by some "boomers" or the older generation directed towards the younger generations called "snowflake". This was a term used to label a sensitive person that expresses their offenses and emotions. Millennials and Generation Z have been actively removing the taboo of talking about their feelings and expressing their emotions. There is an attempt to erase the phrase and action "fake it till you make it" from the vocabulary, and I am happy to hear it. There are moments that we all have to fight through life, and at times it can seem unbearable. Bringing the conversations about mental health to the mainstream is a must in our society so we can all learn how to heal. It is not courageous or makes you a stronger person to willingly fight through the pain and trauma because you can muster through it. It is not a proving ground of the strength of your masculinity and or femininity because you aren't complaining about your issues. No, in fact, it takes courage to confront it, to face it, and get the help you need to win against it. Yes, we bring things to God in prayer, but we can and should also bring things to professionals in the time of help and need. The trauma you choose not to face can be the monster in your closet that that your children will have to learn how to conquer. Depression, anxiety, deep sadness, fear, and all other issues need to be worked through and managed with attention, not avoidance. It's time to speak up, even if it starts at a whisper. You aren't less of a person of faith if you are vocal about your struggles with depression. You aren't less of a man if you talk through your anxiety and learn how to manage it. Speaking up and learning how to talk about the pain and trauma can seem like the hardest step to take.

## Stop Crying

I love being a dad and a husband; it is truly one of the greatest joys in my life. Even before I became a father, I committed that I would never yell at my kids because of the pain and trauma it can cause. I have witnessed the aftermath of this statement as they are crying in my office time and time again, both teenagers and adults alike. This is a phrase that may have been told to you that was told to your parents and so on and so on. A phrase that you may tell your kids and don't think anything of it right before or after you discipline them. The phrase is, "stop crying before I give you something to cry about."

What are we saying to our children when we make that statement depositing those words into their hearts in a high moment of emotional stress? We tell them that their pain doesn't matter, and it is not worth it or justifies the tears in your opinion. Even at toddler ages, we are sowing seeds of separation that will bring the fruit of distance as they grow older, concluding that mom and dad don't care. As parents, we can be emotionally present in the big crisis of our children's lives because we deem it worthy. However, it is the time that their world is shaken that we need to learn how to step down from our high place and perspective to step into their vantage point. It is from that place that we squat low to raise them high. From that place, we are the pioneers to their uncharted waters to lead them out of the emotional struggle to peace and understanding. **You can't yell at your children into peace and ease, but you can yell at them into silence, which is detrimental**. Once the child grows up, they then start to connect the dots separating issues that they can bring to their parents and problems that have to hide from them. Sometimes the belief that someone doesn't care is an assumption, and other times, we can keep giving them reasons that they are correct. We can unintentionally or intentionally raise our kids to compartmentalize pain and trauma. There will be a gradual progression of internalization that sprouts from being a toddler to an adult. It starts with tears flowing, then shifts to holding them back, and ends at a destination to doing whatever the person can do to avoid feeling them at all. Thus, internalized trauma becomes routine, and choosing silence is the background music of their lives.

Did we have the healing process beat out of us and the fear of speaking ingrained in us? Have we been indoctrinated from pain and fear to believe that feeling our feelings is wrong? Each and every one of us needs to take a deep and long look in the mirror. We need to face the person in the mirror head-on and be courageous enough to feel and express how we feel. Depression and anxiety are a mold looking for dark and undisturbed place to grow. We must learn how to speak up and talk about what is happening in our lives to the right people in healthy settings. Maybe you just need an ear to vent to our professional to lead you through, but all of it requires you to open up your mouth.

**Combos**

Depression is a real thing that is hanging on the back of many people. It is a fight that some are facing for the first time, and others have been all of their lives. In this journey together, I introduced some areas that anxiety and depression can stem from and make themselves at home in your life. We talked about Crisis and Trauma and how leaving these issues unchecked can be the breeding ground of a laundry list of issues that you will have to face. Circumstantial depression can come out of nowhere as the crises of life can shake us to our core. The year 2020 can be a testament to that as massive and major circumstances accrued, leaving people homeless, losing businesses, and for many people, dead. When Covid19 hit the USA, Asian communities became victims of hate crimes as hurt, ignorant, and racist people looked for people to hurt, blaming them in the same way americans did to the Muslim communities after September 11$^{th}$ which are unacceptable. I wrote about depression connected to the chemical imbalances we have in our brain that required attention on a biochemical level. If you fall into this category, I hope you have removed the taboo from this area and seek your aid. Whether that is medication, a diet and lifestyle change, or even both, do what you need to do. Many people find it normal for a diabetic person to seek insulin for their chemical imbalances and shift in their diet to aid them; it shouldn't be any different for you getting the help you may require. Lastly, we took the journey to talk about depression coming from spiritual attacks. I am a person of faith. I do believe that the enemy of our soul desires to rob, kill, and destroy. I have a firm belief that Jesus came to step in the gap and carried salvation, healing, and deliverance on His back. But it wasn't written with ink and paper but inscribed using whips and three nails ushering healing and hope. Yet, in addition, as I have already stated, we can completely put our attention in the spiritual realm and give zero attention to what we need to do to move towards health and wellbeing practically. Pray and read, Fast and seek therapy, intercede, and exercise.

In boxing and other fighting sports, there is a term called a "combo"; you chain together multiple punches in one punching segment. Instead of throwing just a single jab, you will throw two jabs, a hook, and finish this with an uppercut. Throwing combos are a great way to land punches and win against your opponent. Could it be in your fight against anxiety and depression you need to throw a combo of healthy community, spirituality, and therapy? Maybe as depression is throwing punches, you need to slip, slip, and counter with two self-care and relaxation hooks. I hope you never find yourself lying on the canvas of depression again because you are fighting back and winning matches. Find a coach or coaches in your life that will walk alongside you that encourage you to talk about your problems.

## The Bell

I am looking forward to the emails and conversations from you telling me that you finally said enough and fought for your peace. I am eager for the moment to see your smile in the airport as you tell me your journey from anxiety and how you are conquering it every day. If you decide to hire me as your Life Coach, I am eager to be a person in the corner of your ring, cheering you on as you excel in life. Look, I know that things have been so hard, and life can throw illegal punches aiming to hit you where it hits the most. But you aren't going to just take it anymore; you are going to be the one taking it to "it." You have every right to speak up and fight for the help you need. I hope depression, anxiety, and all its ugly minions think twice before they dare to stay with you again. You aren't the same person; you are getting trained and learning how to fight and win. The bell is about to ring, and your fight is about to start. Stay behind the jab because it will ensure what you are fighting on the outside of you won't get on the inside you.

# NOTES

# TIMOTHY MCCAIN

# THIS IS YOUR CHANCE

IT'S NOT OPPORTUNITY THAT WILL PASS YOU BY;
IT'S MORE LIKE YOU WILL PASS BY
YOUR OPPORTUNITY

## ABOUT THE AUTHOR

Timothy McCain is a husband and father of two amazing children. He is a thought-leader, life coach, speaker, author, evangelist, content creator, consultant and travels worldwide, sharing hope. He is the author of "Crowns Are Greater Than Trophies" and " This Is Your Chance." Subscribe to his YouTube Channel, and Podcast called "TMMotivations".

www.TimothyMcCain.com
www.TMMonline.org
www.TMMOasis.com
Twitter: @TimothycwMcCain
Instagram: @Timothy_McCain

Made in USA - North Chelmsford, MA
1231859_9781736520000
02.24.2021 1614